Published in Australia

by Parris

Postal 6/2 Manningham St. Parkville 3052 Victoria

Tel. +61 434 094 377

First printed in Australia 2015

Copyright Parris © 2015

National library of AustraliaCataloguing -in-

GOD SAVE AFRICA

ISBN 978-0-9945123-1-4

Layout and design by Parris

Printed by Ingram Sparks

Typeset in Palatino !!pt on 11pt

Disclaimer

All care has been taken in the production of the information herein but no responsibility can be accepted by the publisher or author for any damage resulting from the misinterpretation of this work.

GOD SAVE AFRICA
Jill Parris

Dedicated to those who still hope for
a
South Africa for all

My dearest children,

I write this to be read on your twenty first birthday because I want you to understand why I was not able to fulfil my deepest desire to be a hands on dad. As you know I grew up without a father so understand how difficult this can be.

My father died in the pursuit of South Africa's freedom from Apartheid. His dream seemed to be realised when Mandela became our president. However this slowly faded as the ANC started to put themselves ahead of their people.

As a reporter I was engaged in trying to keep the dream alive but when this became too dangerous your mother and I decided that she would take you out of the country.

I am pleased with how well you have settled and integrated into your new home.

I love the people you have become but am overwhelmed with sadness that I had so little to do with your growing up years. The choice was mine. Your loss of connection with Africa and your heritage was the result. I am sorry.

If only South Africans had been prepared to take democracy back while they had the chance.

That is now past and it is time for you to hear the whole story.

Love

Tata.

Introduction

I expected the clatter of sadness but not the constant refrain of "things were better under Apartheid."

How does a country start again after such a scourge?

I fled life under South Africa's Apartheid thirty-five years ago with no hope that the Nationalist government would ever lose power. In Australia we were invited to support Umkhonto we Sizwe the then banned armed wing of the African National Congress in its mission to fight against the South African government. We did not, because, while in sympathy with their political stance, we as pacifists believe it is not right to support violence even in defence of constitutional reform.

Having made this decision we threw ourselves into establishing new lives, contributing where we could to community in Australia, but returning occasionally to our beloved South Africa to visit family and friends.

After retiring from fulfilling careers, Dave and I decided to return to Kalk Bay, the place where I'd enjoyed childhood holidays, with a clearly defined project brief. With David's help I would interview Apartheid's so called "Coloured people." My name for them was the "forgotten people" because it seemed to me, as an ex-"white", that under this ridiculous classification system for the peoples of South Africa the Coloured's had always seemed to miss out.

My project went effortlessly with each interviewee happy to address my question

Is it better now than under Apartheid?

Most asked what I meant by "the forgotten people", laughing at my "well, were you consulted on anything?"

About half way through the project though, I went to interview a man who was not "coloured" and who told me plainly that an associate had been affronted by this "label."

This was but one of several confrontations I faced in this meeting; hard to hear but very productive in outcome.

For the first time I knowingly faced my own prejudices in relation to "colour and classification", the cornerstone of Apartheid, and realised to my immense horror that I am nothing more than a product of my white South African heritage. I fall clearly into the "privileged white do-gooder clan."

This for me was a turning point in my project. I could not undo what I had begun, but what I could do was broaden my scope to include anyone who came across my path that was interested in this work. Not very scientific, but a decision which brought new voices into the conversation.

My pool extended and my listening deepened but the question remained the same. My time spent with people was always longer than an hour and often included second visits and the sharing of meals.

The twenty-five people I interviewed in Cape Town and the Western Cape, from a variety of backgrounds, ethnicities and walks of life, were all warm, open and generous. But what they told me was that twenty-one years after the fall of the Nationalist government in South Africa, a still divided society felt worse off, not better.

"At least under Apartheid we knew where we stood. Today the government makes promises but does nothing."

For them a litany of issues affect their everyday lives. Poverty, unemployment, homelessness and inadequate housing, an ailing public health system, inadequate and ageing infrastructure, poor education and, most importantly, corruption both within and outside of government make life difficult, dangerous and unpredictable.

When these everyday occurrences are overlaid with the continual social ills of violence, both within families and in the broader community, crime, drugs and AIDS, life becomes a daily struggle for survival.

And now to the new theme that underlies this project. South Africa is a country at war with itself.

"No wonder we see xenophobia. It's almost a relief to have someone to blame."

And so to the novella that has come from these experiences.

"We have had the military deployed to the townships before, using the tactics employed by the National Party is not going to solve the challenges the country is facing, this will not solve the problems creating unrest,"

Moeletsi Mbeki
24 April 2015

TABLE OF CONTENTS

Map of Cape Peninsula

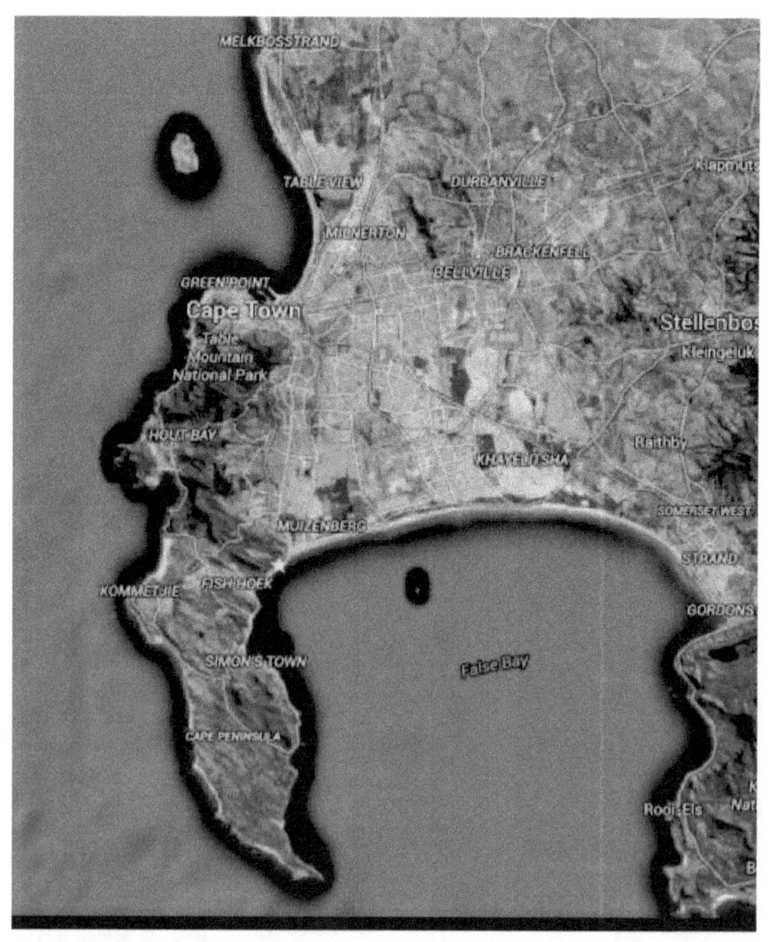

NO FUTURE WITHOUT FORGIVENESS

Cape Town Talks

"South Africa belongs to the Khoi-San people, everyone else is a visitor."

Themba looks over the partition between his and the next sterile, soundproofed, formica stall at the rest of this nondescript windowless office. He can scarcely breathe. His swivel chair hardly contains his loose long limbed body, so he stands, stretches to his full one meter ninety, runs his spare fingers over his forehead and through his whorl of black peppercorns. How long will he survive in this place? "I'm a man of action not a damn sounding board for crazy women, I should be out there, grabbing the latest stories and selling my slant to the world. Not listening to ranting know-it-all callers."

"If each person remembered that all but the Khoi San were invaders, there would be less to argue about when it came to Xenophobia."

Cape Town Talking's quota man is taken aback. He puts the crazy lady on hold and connects another call. She's still there after an intense discussion about yet another murder, this time of a Mozambican family man by four men in Johannesburg's Alexandra Township. When will this horrendous killing spree stop? Then it's her turn. He puts the caller through to Nalendi, turns from the switchboard, and listens intently. After all, if he's to laugh with his friends about her outrageous claims he needs to understand what she's on about. She speaks first about how the Khoi-San roamed the Cape before either European or Bantu settlement.

"We welcomed white settlers, they first walked into our land and then all over us. Both sides have literally raped us. Black people have raped Khoi-San people, and white people have raped Khoi-San people. I am a direct descendant of one such union and I'm saying, acknowledge who we are, and give back what is rightfully ours. We are the only Aboriginal people. If you accepted that you came as invaders you would not attack those who come here from outside South Africa as easily, black or white."

"Who the hell does she think she is?"

After two weeks in the job he's now getting the hang of settling angry, sad and even patronising callers but somehow this "lady" irritates him more then most. How dare she question the status quo? It has taken South Africa so long to recognise the blacks and here she is directly contradicting this fact.

But then, as he listens Themba is drawn in. He hates that his position is a sinecure, he hates that the ANC, his government, has become a kleptocracy and he hates the ongoing violence that dogs his country. He remembers as a little boy listening to his mother wonder at the New South Africa where all people could be free. He remembers her excitement at the new constitution. "When did it all go wrong? If only I could do something to make a difference."

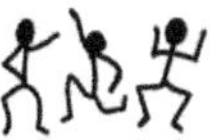

The past three months have been a whirlwind. Themba got his job in late January, had a weeks training in Johannesburg and then left his young family to see if he could make a go of it in Cape Town. Nomalisa is to follow with the two year old twins once he is settled.

Everyone at work is superficially friendly but standoffish. He has settled into a share house in Elsie's River okay but Themba had not counted on the impact of the news on his life. So much has happened since he joined the radio station.

First there was the triple axe murder on the Cape Flats. This drug related killing spree was reported as one of many. Themba is used to carnage, but somehow it is much worse hearing caller's responses than reading about murders in the paper. Here the violence has an impact on staff, on callers and on him. In fact it sort of hangs in the air. Everyone is on tenterhooks, the calls just keep coming and all and sundry have something to say. "Tik is what's behind it. When you get high you get angry, aggressive and lose all inhibition." Everyone is reminded again that the Cape Flats is a zone of extreme danger, almost a war zone in fact and despite South Africa's high crime rates the government does nothing.

And then there are the fires. Immediately Cape Town Talks finds itself drawn into the drama. Almost all of the Cape Peninsular is alight and it goes on for weeks. This knocks the talk of murder off the airwaves. The fires are scary but they are also a threat to everyone and draw all the attention.

They start in the early hours of Sunday, 1 March 2015 on the mountain behind Muizenberg and spread quickly because of extremely high temperatures and strong winds. Within a couple of days they have spread right across the mountain to the West coast. Members of the public in affected areas are advised to hose down thatched roofs and keep all windows closed.

The fire fighting effort draws staff and volunteers from all around the Western Cape.

By Wednesday, one fire fighter has sustained burn wounds and is in hospital and fifty-two frail care residents are being treated for smoke inhalation.

Then five homes are burned to the ground and a lodge is damaged. At least thirty households and two retirement homes are evacuated and three mass care centres are set up to accommodate the displaced.

People keep phoning CTT wanting updates and it is our job to keep Cape Town connected. When it becomes evident that fire-fighting services are stretched beyond their limits, we set up a pledge line to raise money for much needed resources and equipment. The lines ring constantly and I hardly draw breath. CTT is buzzing.

It is great to be part of a team rushed off our feet helping. Everyone here and in the community is pulling together. An emergency brings out the best in everyone. There are the complaints that the Democratic Alliance, who run the Western Cape, have allowed emergency services to run down, but we are all used to the knockers. I lose track of myself, submerged in the joint work effort and for a couple of weeks forget that I am the outsider who can't pull his weight, and I love it.

But like all good things, the fire is extinguished and CTT moves on.

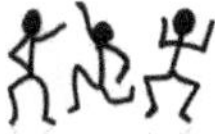

Themba moves through the stuffy train bound for his rented room in Elsies River. At last a break from the all consuming compassion demanded by the worst mountain fire in a decade.

He can't believe his luck as he finds a seat in an empty carriage, slumps down, shuts his eyes and unwinds in syncopated solitude.

The sound of the train deepens into a drumbeat and stamping feet, and Themba circles the flaming bonfire beside his impi brothers. Red dust rises and smoke fills the air as the flames rise to meet the star filled heaven. The hypnotic hammer of bare feet welcomes the ancestors to join the chanting initiates as they sing and stamp their path to manhood.

> *Shaka, Zulu, impi, man*
> *Brother, hunter, soldier stand*
> *With the ANC man by man*
> *Together for our nation, land.*
> *Shaka, Zulu, impi, man.*

The drumbeat hammers and the stamping feet echo the rhythm into the black firmament. All Zulu men must stand together in united support of their king and community.

Whatever Themba does, wherever he goes, he is Zulu first. He lives for his brother, his nation his land. Together they are strong. From generation to generation their strength comes from acting as clan, supporting their cause and king. Zulu men act as one. They stand, fight and vote as a block. Strong and proud in the path of their ancestors who watch and guide from beyond the grave. Every fibre of Themba the man throbs to this collective Zulu heartbeat.

As I live and breathe

A Zulu man I stand

With Shaka, Zulu, impi, Man

Then without interruption the sound sharpens into the thrashing beat of a helicopter cutting ark upon ark between shimmering sea, opaque sky and burning mountain as it scoops water from the harbour and dumps it on fire with sound shattering monotony. Scoop, rise, dump, rise, scoop, rise, dump until leaping flames are subsumed in palls of acrid yellow smoke hanging heavy in the air. The air is still, hot and heavy with smoke but occasionally a small patch clears to reveal stark skeletons and scorched slopes in the place of green mountain scrub.

Themba tastes the dust, smoke and desolation, gasps to catch his breath and slumps forward as he is jolted from his reverie by shrieking wheels. The train stops.

Now clammy bodies pile into his carriage and consciousness.

A young man slumps down beside him, and two others take the seat across and facing him. Themba moves to accommodate the newcomers but does not open his eyes.

The man next to him speaks "Finally the fire is out."

Themba does not raise his gaze but tunes in. He is interested.

"So the mountain burns, a few white houses are damaged and the world pays attention."

"Yes I heard that both CNN and the BBC have been covering the Cape Town fires. They claim that these are the worst for a decade. I'm so sick of this. How often have lives been lost to fire in Khayelitsha with no response from anyone?"

"Ya! Remember last year four children were trapped in their house and burned to death at their front door unable to open or escape because they were locked in; and the four thousand homeless after the shack fires of 2013. Those incidents barely raised a mention in the local rag. But when the mountain burns and one or two rich white buggers need to take shelter the world knows all about it."

"Nothing will ever change in this country. It will always be the Whites who are looked after and we the non-white masses are jettisoned and barely survive and continue unnoticed."

"Well this is South Africa. We have our black government now but nothing has changed. Our wonderful ANC mates who saved our nation from Apartheid now believe the spoils of government are theirs and we are left as before to slave for nothing or die in poverty."

"Khayelitsha wouldn't even exist if they hadn't bussed us in from the Eastern Cape to vote them in and now we live where they promised us houses under sheets of corrugated iron.

As Themba slips back into sleep the beat of the wheels take on words.

Shacks burn down in Khayelitsha
No-one cares, no Sunday Feature
Just skollies, drugs, no SAP
No-go zone for you and me

Shipped in by the ANC
To set the Western Province free
Promised houses, jobs and schools
No jobs, no houses, we just fools

Iron lean-tos, side by side
Tinder waiting for a braai
Khayalitsha shacks burn easy
Life is cheap. Don't waste a sigh

Who will go there? No not me
I am Zulu, ANC
Not like refuse from PE
Who vote DA and think they're free

The wheels screech again and I wake to see the Tygerburg Hospital stop, the one after mine. I rise, alight and trudge the extra ten blocks back to my room, a shower and bed. As I walk through the humid smoke filled pall that has blown off the mountain I wonder what tomorrow will bring.

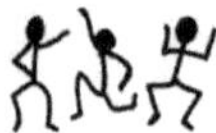

The next big thing to hit us is talk of the Rhodes statue on the Cape Town University campus. At a protest on the tenth of March the leaders fling human waste on the statue, calling for its removal. "This poo we are throwing on the statue represents the shame of black people . . . we are throwing our shame to whites' affluence. As black students at UCT we have to change our ways just to fit in, keep quiet . . . Its time for change. We are disgusted by the fact that this statue still stands here symbolising white supremacy."

I have to say I am appalled. Don't those guys know how lucky they are to be at UCT? I would have given my back teeth to go there. Yes, Rhodes was an imperialist. We all know that. But even if he did say that he would "build the university out of the kafirs' stomach" do we have to be offensive just because he was? I agree that the statue has "great symbolic power" and glorifies someone "who exploited black labour and stole land from indigenous people."

But when the protest leaders started saying that South Africa's "so called" miraculous transition to democracy in 1994 was a failure whereas the removal of Rhodes statue from the UCT campus is a marker of true transition, I am mortified, and when I hear that they are chanting "one settler one bullet" I become angry. Aren't we beyond this? Do we have to sink to that level? After all the ANC has been in power for twenty-one years now. Surely our government needs to take some responsibility for what is going on in this country.

It is clear that there are still many problems, but don't we need the statue there to remind us that our struggle is far from over? Shouldn't such icons be kept, as reminders of where we have come from and how far we still have to go?

I am still pondering my position when Nalendi pulls me aside saying we at CTT lead commentary on the news. "Make sure no caller hears your opinions, whatever they are." Again the shame! I can feel myself blush.

These feelings stay with me for days. I have always been torn between believing in myself as a proud Zulu warrior and feeling I will never make it in my own right. After all a couple of CTT staff have told me directly that Nalendi wanted to employ a white girl with superior skills but had gone with me because they had to take on their token black man first. Each time I hear them muttering about "racism in reverse" I cringe.

Still caught up in my inadequacies and the ongoing statue stuff I am bowled over by the latest news from Natal. Apparently Goodwill Zwelithini, my king, has fuelled the already seething emotions among my people, the Zulus, by saying "when you walk down the street you can't recognise a shop you used to know because it has been taken over by foreigners who mess it up by hanging up rags. They should be deported." His suggestion has added fuel to the smouldering embers of xenophobia. In running battles in Durban's city centre, the wail of sirens has filled the air, tear gas and rubber bullets have been fired and a 14-year-old boy is among those who died in the attacks. Six or more foreigners were killed in separate incidents.

The ravages of Xenophobia now overtake normal programming at CTT. How can we contribute to rebuilding calm in our frazzled country? Well, immediately we do what we have been trained to do in any difficult situation. We listen.

Off air we glean as much information as we can. At first many foreigners are so afraid that they flee South Africa and several African neighbours challenge the Government about allowing Xenophobia to raise its ugly head again.

Immediately proposals are made to confine foreigners in refugee camps, to tighten border controls, ban foreign businesses and land ownership, or to ban foreigners altogether.

The Government steps in fairly rapidly, and despite lingering unease they are credited with dealing with the violence more swiftly than they did the attacks against migrants in 2008. This time they have not left civil society to take the lead in working to end the violence.

However one advocacy group says the government's latest response has shown an attempt to divert attention from its failure to deal with unemployment and inequality. They add that beneath the appeals for tolerance there are also calls to bring the issue to a swift close.

Religious leaders, both Christian and Muslim, work hard to calm their followers and call for an end to Xenophobia by quoting scripture "You shall neither mistreat a stranger, nor oppress him" and "love your neighbour, and do to others what you would want them to do to you."

Many also reminded followers of Madiba's words "to deny people their human rights is to challenge their very humanity."

We are also reminded of the work of the truth and Reconciliation Commission and as I listen to an interview with Desmond Tutu my back straightens and I lean forward gripped by his words

"The reason for the commission shining a light on the past was precisely to contribute to the processes of national healing and ensure that we never committed such foul deeds again."

"Yet here we are, less than a generation later, witnessing hate crimes on a par with the worst that Apartheid could offer. I will pray for the perpetrators of xenophobic violence just as I prayed for PW Botha and his security forces; that their eyes may be opened and they see the fault of their ways."

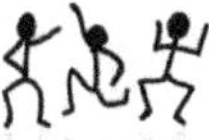

I am inspired by these words, and in CTT's briefing meetings I now forget my cynical protective shell, listen and am alert and open to each new idea. I want to be part of the solution.

But alas when we are back on air I am reminded of my status as gatekeeper and assistant, an outsider, and armour up again. It is my job to have callers backed up and waiting to go on, not to interact with those who ring in.

Still, I cannot help hearing what this caller says, "This country belongs to the Khoi-San, everyone else is just a visitor." My neck stiffens and my jaw tightens but then, as I begin to understand that what she says is true, my tension shifts. Her people have been violated by both black and white.

I have suffered under Apartheid but is it possible to be both violated under Apartheid and also an aggressor? I go hot and cold. My mouth goes dry. Never before have I looked at my responsibilities as a South African. Mandela led us into a new dispensation. He said again and again that everyone must be equally protected and it sounds like the Khoi-San are not recognised as the first people. I certainly feel sad for them. What should I do?

By the time Nalendi comes off air I am babbling. "We should be doing more to change what is happening. Remember what Tutu said about the Truth and Reconciliation Commission. I remember watching it on telly night after night for years as a boy. He said 'If only we can bring ordinary people together to share their hurt, maybe things can change.' How can we do more than listen? How can we contribute to bringing people together?"

Themba's childhood

I am numb as I think about my Dad. I can't remember him at all but I remember the stories. He was a teacher at the high school in Impedle and one day he went to a meeting in Howick and did not return. I was not yet five years old. I was not told what happened, but often overheard talk of Inkatha and the ANC being at war with each other. Whenever I asked my mother she would turn away in tears and say, "Politics leads to terrible trouble but such things are not for the ears of children. Know, Themba, that you are the oldest son and your job is to grow big and strong so that you can support your little sister Sizani and me in your father's place. We cannot live with your grandmother Gogo for ever."

Soon after this Noxolo, my 'mother of peace', left us in Gogo's care and travelled to Johannesburg, the city of gold, to work as a housemaid in the home of a rich Jewish businessman. Before she left she took me aside "remember Themba it is your job to help with Sizani. She is walking now so you must watch her well because she will be running all over the place soon. And you my son will be attending school before I can return. Promise me you will be diligent in your schoolwork and help with Sizani. On weekends you will be able to herd cattle like all the other boys in the village, and you must help your grandfather Umkhulu to till the land, cultivate crops and harvest them. Remember milking cows, feeding the pigs and the chickens is also a young man's work. Now stay well my son. I will send money home for you and Sizani. Never forget that I am your mother and I love you." With this Noxolo hugged both Themba and Sizani close and took her leave.

I was to begin school in the year I turned six and Noxolo left in late 1989 when I was still five. I had a wonderful winter and spring wandering the folded foothills below the imposing Drakensburg and can still feel my simmering resentment at being contained at school between seven and two. Noxolo had emphasised the imperative of school. "Your father was proud of his education and loved being a teacher. One day you can follow him and finish what he started. Learning brings freedom." Umkhulu on the other hand taught me "your roots are in the Zulu impis. You must learn like all true men that discipline and bravery are essential. We are soldiers like our ancestor Shaka the founder of the Zulu nation. You have big feet to fill."

Noxolo was gone for a long time and Sizani learned to turn to me for comfort. I remember still her small voice "Ba sore" and tears of pain or frustration. I liked that she saw me as big and strong. It felt reassuring to have another depend on me. For her I was special. I was busy during the day but at night I would put her down to sleep and sing Noxolo's Tula lullaby just as she had sung to me. I loved it when she cuddled close and called me Ba and I often fell asleep on her mat. We always ate breakfast together before I went to school or into the hills with the cattle.

When at last Noxolo came back for a visit Sizani ran off crying and hid. "No! you go." She didn't know her at all. When Noxolo finally persuaded Sizani to come close she clung to us both and cried "I promise it will not be so long again."

From then on I would travel to Saxonwold, Johannesburg, with Sizani for our Christmas holidays and we would stay in the servants quarters or play in the wonderful big yard. The Goldblatts, Noxolo's employers would be away in Plettenburg Bay for a substantial part of our stay but when they were home Barney, their only son, just a little older than me would say "come play tennis" or "let's swim." Swimming was always a problem as Sizani couldn't keep her head above water and screamed "drowning, save me, drowning" if allowed in the water, and if shut out of the pool area "let me in I want swim." But I loved tennis. Of course Noxolo was always busy. "It is my job to cook or clean so you must watch Sizani."

Barney and I would also play cricket in the driveway or sit together with Sizani between us and watch our team prepare for cricket games overseas. I constantly asked "why's it such a big deal Barney" and he would reply "now the boycotts are over we can play overseas and prove that we are best in the world."

Barney's mother, whom I called Mam, told me "your English is poor, Themba. Come into the kitchen, sit down at the table. I want you to learn good elocution." At first I wriggled uncomfortably not able to shape my mouth around the words but then Barney said "when she did it with me I pretended I was a parrot" and I was able to do this with ease. Now Mam said my "diction improved by leaps and bounds." Sizani would sit still and upright next to me during these lessons, moving her mouth but uttering no sound and her English also progressed well despite her silence. She was a smart kid, and I was as proud of her as any mother would be.

In the times between visiting Noxolo, life was mostly routine. I'd begin days with school and in the afternoons join the other young boys in the hills between the village and the mountain to heard cattle.   Mostly these days were pleasant and uneventful but one afternoon still sets my heart racing. We had driven the cattle towards a valley where crystal water spilled across silver grey rocks into a deep black pool. Here we stripped and swam shrieking with joy at our liberty, oblivious of a building storm. A crack of thunder and knife of lightening struck a rock directly below us and towards our village. Without considering our charges we all scrambled rapidly towards an overhanging crevice to the side and above us. Once sheltered, we shivered with fright and rubbed warmth into our skinny naked bodies as we squinted out across the valley through a sheet of rain. Water began dripping down the walls of the overhang. "What will we do?"

"Wait for the rain to stop."

I looked up. As the wall became wet patterns emerged. Then strange figures appeared. "Look here is a man on his back with a stick going through him . . . No it's an assegai and another and over here, bigger figures chasing the smaller ones with spears . . . and above the dead man there is this sort of eland with wings . . . Can you see?"

"I wonder who did these?"

We returned to the village shivering and soaked to the skin several hours later. When Gogo had finished punishing me she looked into my wide eyes and asked, "What have you seen that has shocked you so?" When I told her about the paintings on the rock walls she smiled. "Many years ago there was a battle between the evil little mountain people and our warriors. They would stalk and kill our cattle with their bows and poisoned arrows. Our king Cetshwayo sent his impis to drive them from our land." Our bedraggled cattle returned at milking time."

As I grew I struggled more with going to Saxonwold. I felt inside out in the city. In Impedle I spent most of my time with other boys my age. At school we would learn and laugh and make mischief together and in the afternoons we would roam with the cattle in hills. We were not yet men but we had freedom. But in Johannesburg it was different. I was confined to the servant's quarters and back yard unless in Barney's company, and was not allowed out on the street. And Sizani was always with me. Noxolo expected me to be serious and to be adaptable. "South Africa is changing my son. Mr Mandela is out of prison and the Boers are talking to him. You must prepare to take your place. Listen well to Mam she knows about the new politics and she is always telling me that soon we will have the vote. So stand straight my son and do as Mam asks when she gives you tasks. But most of all listen and learn. I only know the old ways but you will be free and you must do this right. You are blessed my son."

I was almost ten when South Africa had its first democratic election. For the first time all races in the country went to the polls to vote for a government of their choosing. From the beginning of that school year our teachers had talked about little else. They said that our national hero Nelson Mandela, who had grown up in a valley just like ours, became a lawyer and fought for his people against Apartheid. He and other brave men had been sent to prison but after twenty-seven years he had now been released and was speaking to the Boers about power and freedom for our people. There was a new excitement in our village but also fear, and Gogo told me "if there is trouble at any time take Sizani, Themba and run into the mountains for your safety. And always protect your sister. When there is danger it is often the women and girls who get hurt."

On the 27th April 1994 I had no school. Instead I went with Gogo, who shuffled along in the longest queue I had ever seen. It snaked backwards and forwards along the streets of Impedle then down across the river and back some way towards the mountain. I rushed up and down the line with my mates; skipping, laughing and squealing as we resonated with the effervescent excitement of delighted voters. This was the first time I had seen black and white people standing alongside each other. I watched open mouthed as everyone gossiped together as they wrung joy out of each moment of this momentous occasion, their first opportunity to vote together in the freedom of a fully franchised election.

There had been warnings of trouble on Election Day, so Gogo had risen early to escape the crowds, but she was not the only one with this idea. Hundreds had already joined the queue.

Later Gogo said, "I could not believe that this day could come." What was more amazing to her was that she who "had never chatted happily with a white person" had talked openly with white people about the New South Africa. "I did not cast my vote until late that evening and I have never been as proud as when I made my cross for Mr Mandela on that ballot paper. This has been the best day of my life."

I know that countless people struggled over many years for our new democracy and it was a fight well fought and won, but for me it offered little but confusion. My life did not change but expectations seemed higher.

Noxolo had always been pleased with my schoolwork but now Mam told her I needed to improve my standard of reading and writing because I would need to compete in a "bigger world." She gave me books to read when back in the village between visits, but there were no lights to read by at night and my days were full. Anyway I was never interested in books. My life was too full of adventure to sit still and read. I became resentful. "Umkhulu is getting old and he needs more help. I need to do his work Ma. When do I have time to read?"

When I was twelve I refused to leave Impedle for the holidays. Sizani, who also found Joburg a drag, said "Ma I am also needed in the village. It's where I belong with the girls and women of the village."

"OK, I will came home for visits when I can." In fact she managed only a few brief visits. "They need me in Joburg. I'm sorry my children."

At fourteen my friends and I were initiated into manhood and became warriors of the Zulu nation. We were taken off to a secret place, were taught Zulu folk law and tradition and had our foreskins removed. Much of what I was taught is forgotten but I still remember the agony inflicted by circumcision that stayed with me for what seemed like a very long time.

As a man I was expected to seek employment and Gogo suggested "you must return to Saxonwold to look for work. There is nothing here for you. You will need to go and find money in the city of gold." I was now fifteen and had completed year eight but without passing all my subjects. "Go. You can live with Noxolo, find work and study in the evening."

Unfortunately when I arrived in Joburg there were more job seekers than work, and Mam did not like me "loitering around the house", so I'd skulk out of sight when she was around. I spent many indigent hours walking from house to house in nearby suburbs looking for gardening jobs but without success. Shopkeepers were also not interested in me, saying

"You look sloppy and have no skills. Finish your schooling and perhaps you will have more to offer."

I was not sure where else to look, so often sat depressed, lonely and bored in front of the television in Noxolo's room. Broadcasts of the Truth and Reconciliation Commission offered real life drama and held my attention. In my angrier moments I would fantasise about those who had rejected me as a worker having to answer to the TRC about their cruel rejection of my service.

One evening as I was watching the TRC, Noxolo came into her room, stood dead still for a couple of minutes and then let out a stifled groan. Tears stained her cheeks, as she stood transfixed by what she saw. A Kwa-Zulu policeman was talking about an incident in which his colleagues had murdered a group of workmates who refused to cover up Inkatha's criminal activity. I put my arms around her and she sobbed into my shoulder. "We will never know what happened my son. He kept his political activities to himself but I was told that your father was a martyr to the cause. I loved him and I miss him so."

After months of sneaking in and out of the Saxonwold property, often aided by Barney who hated his mother's hypocrisy, I decided to move to Soweto. My idea was to find a way of finishing high school and also to get help with looking for work. Not so easy. Unemployment was endemic. Noxolo gave me a little cash, which helped, but people laughed when I asked about finding work. "The Boers are leaving, so work is hard to find especially if you can't read and write fluently. You have to learn to look after yourself."

While many well off South Africans were emigrating in the late 1990's refugees were flooding into the country from the north and those who came from Zimbabwe, our closest neighbour, were better educated than those of us who had grown up with the third class education reserved for blacks under Apartheid. We were angry that they came into our country and stole our jobs, and this fuelled many Xenophobic attacks across the country. I, like other job seekers, began to resent the intrusion from the north.

I walked into the dilapidated church come job centre, filled in some paperwork and went up to a counter. A dead-eyed old man looked past me and gave me a number. "Wait over there."

"How long?"

He shrugged. "Next."

I huffed out to find the lines end, sat, scuffed at the ground with my shabby shoe, cursed under my breath and looked around. A lanky spiv came up and smiled. "Looks like you got time to spare hey. Bloody long queue. Can I help?"

"I need work now."

"Well, we need a guard. Want to meet my men and talk?"

"Sure."

Mr Spiv pulled me to my feet and headed down a dusty lane. My heart beat faster as I picked up pace and followed. Maybe I'd just made a huge mistake. I slowed and Spiv slowed too.

"Coming?" I wasn't sure. "OK man, this is it." He pushed a door open and we walked into a noisy, dark, smoke filled room. "Hey guys this here is Legs, our new guard."

An old guy handed me a beer. "Tom" he said. "Where you from man?"

"Around here" I answered in the direction of the voice, too scared now to concentrate. A woman's voice sizzled

"I not seen ye Good Looking, couldn't have been around for long."

"OK" said Spiv, "You look creeped out my man, let's just take this one step at a time. All you got to do is hang out on the corner and whistle if someone comes and for this you get to stay with us, have a meal and a bed. Once we knew we can trust you we'll talk money."

Sweating and with my tongue dry, too frightened to say no, I said yes. We hung out until dark and then I was led through back streets to the 'main scene'.

"OK Legs, you hang here. Whistle if anyone comes. We'll be about ten." I leant against the wall shivering in fright but no one came until the guys returned pockets bulging. "OK let's go." We walked off. I was given a meal and a bed and told that I was in. Spiv smiled as I went off to sleep. "It'll be easier next time Legs!"

I joined the Sunnies and we did burglaries in and around the wealthier parts of Soweto. I was watchman for a couple of months but then graduated to doing break-ins. Life was easy and I loved the rush of outwitting my adversaries, the spoilt, cool apparatchiks, well prepared to jump into the high paid pencil pushing jobs that came as the ANC's spoils of new government.

I did some burgs on the side to supplement my growing needs and particularly enjoyed depending only on myself. That was until I happened upon an old lady and found myself threatening her with a chisel.

"The old lady lives alone now. Her son was killed in the mines," said Tom. "Get in quick, grab the compo money and get out. She'll go to sleep early."

I prepared well. Put on my black clothes and balaclava and left my pushbike around the corner for a quick get away. This was different to the burgs we did as a gang but it sounded easy. "An old lady on her own. You know what you're doing and you not scared any more. You been with us three years now."

I pushed hard at the door and it started to give way. A quick whack with my chisel and I was in. I stopped a moment and looked around. Two bedrooms, a living space and a kitchen but perhaps more cluttered than usual. This lady was well looked after. I heard nothing but the tick of a clock. "She must be in bed like Tom said."

I walked through the dark lounge and into the kitchen and stood a moment. Not a whisper. I turned on my torch and headed over to the stove. That's where the old dears usually hide their money. Chisel in hand, just in case, I headed for the oven. The money would be there behind the element. I was just about to open the oven door when I heard a sound.

I turned and shone my torch towards the sound and saw an old lady cringing on a chair at a table in the corner next to the door. I raised my chisel and took a step towards her. Just one thud to the back of her head and she'd be gone. "Should be in bed old lady!" She looked up at me as I moved in for the kill.

"What are you doing my son?"

I took a step to the side to get the angle right and then froze. Maybe it was the change of angle but what I saw wasn't any old lady, it was Gogo. "Oh shit what am I doing?' Suddenly overwhelmed by self-loathing I dropped my hand, cried "Sorry Gogo" and fled empty handed and shocked at what I had become. My three year crime spree had come to an abrupt end.

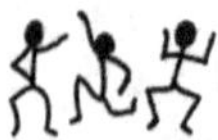

Exhausted and humiliated I went back to my mother and asked, "Help me Ma." She in turn went to Mam who offered to get me into Damelin College. I would pay her back by working in the garden.

This was the breakthrough I needed. I studied hard and worked in the garden on weekends. I did well enough to pass my high school certificate.

At Damelin I met Nomalisa in a communications course. We became project buddies, working together on developing a dummy outreach program to rehabilitate street gangs in Soweto, and found that our skills worked well together. I of course knew the street gang mentality first hand and Nomalisa was a generous and deeply caring person who just knew how to put things so that people would be inspired by our message. When we presented in class we had our whole cohort cheering. "You guys are daunting." Each student said they would join our outreach program and get behind our message anytime. In fact one of them suggested "why don't we trial it as a class?" We got the highest grade for that project.

Now Nomalisa and I spent every lunchtime together. We would take our subsidised meal out onto the lawn and eat and share stories of our childhood. Nomalisa had always lived in Soweto and had taken responsibility for her siblings at twelve. "When my father left with another woman my mum fell apart. She couldn't cope, so I took over. The little ones were scared so I just got on with it. Someone had to take responsibility so I did. I like to care for others." As I listened and looked into her eyes I saw my own soul mirrored in their depth. This woman was a better version of me, a soul mate. As we spoke or studied together in the sun I became more and more bewitched by this angel. She filled my world with light and laughter. She understood my sadness, she sometimes spoke sentences before I had formulated them in my mind. I began to feel that I did not know where she ended and I began, and the magic between us grew and electrified as we met always in public and did no more than hold hands and gaze at each other. We were both too restrained to break our connection through becoming physical.

Finally, however, we were both so frantic that we had to admit it. "I love you Themba." Nomalisa said to me one afternoon as we stood together before going our separate ways.

"And I you my beloved!"

We were in love and had to consummate our commitment. Touching hands and gazing into each other's eyes was no longer enough, so we found a room in Soweto and moved in together. "Nomalisa, I love you and want to make love to you forever." For days and nights we were consumed only in each other. "You my woman are my all in all."

Now what I had only guessed about Nomalisa was unveiled. She was more than the caring person I knew, she was truly committed to serving society. All her spare time, which was little, was spent working at a voluntary job with AIDS victims. "These women and children are our people and they are dying. There is no choice. The work is simply there to be done. My studies are a way into becoming a nurse so that I can live out my commitment to them."

Nomalisa spent endless hours educating and treating HIV infected mothers and their babies. At the time Thabo Mbeki, Mandela's replacement as president, denied the link between HIV and AIDS and recommended the use of herbal remedies to treat the disease. This meant that getting antiretroviral drugs was difficult. Many people died and her fury at the government's refusal to listen to modern science fuelled Nomalisa determination to expose his folly. She spoke about the issue often at school and began a support group to spread the word. She brought students to her clinic and introduced them to the program. "You must see for yourselves how the policies of our president actually kill people." Many joined the volunteer team and our lecturer took it upon herself to create a couple of assignments that also highlighted the plight of AIDS victims more widely. The department came on board and more funds flowed to the project. My Nomalisa was a star.

But this was not enough for Nomalisa. She wanted the world to know what was happening. She invited several foreign correspondents to the centre. "Please come and find out what is happening first hand." They immediately became interested and added reporting on the AIDS crisis to their list of musts. On board, they now wanted to take the issues to the world so that pressure from outside countries, and hopefully the UN, could compel Mbeki to rethink his approach. Through Nomalisa I met one journalist who simply blew my mind. His excitement at being able to influence others through his writing awoke in me a longing to do likewise.

With a reasonable school leaving I was able to get a night shift job as a cashier at a garage not far out of Soweto, so after Damelin I enrolled at a local college as a journalism student. At college I met and made my first real friendships outside my impi brothers.

Now for the first time in my life I worked at having fun. I had loved drumming as a youth and when I was not working would join my college mates at the local shebeen and play in a makeshift band. Nomalisa would come along and sing if she had any time free from her AIDS work. She sang slow,seductive love songs, aimed only at me I hoped, in a resonant, honey filled, deep alto which not only blew me away but also wowed and won over everyone else who listened. My heart would leap and my drumming become slow and seductive. Our music became yet another pathway into the depths of our loving.

We were also mad soccer fans and watched matches whenever we had a chance. When the world cup came to South Africa we were swept up in its fever and while we couldn't get into the stadium for the Soweto match we joined the throngs who watched and cheered in front of one of the big screens erected in many public places. "All eyes are on us. The world is here and we are in their living rooms. How wonderful to feel we are part of the world and they are watching us as a nation." We blew our vuvuzelas with the rest of our countrymen, smiled and sang our national anthem. "Nkosi Sikelel' iAfrika. God bless Africa." We also made sure that all was calm and crime free.

Our lives were full, effusive and living was overwhelmingly consuming until Nomalisa came to me one day "I am pregnant."

"What?"

"I'm having our baby."

"But we haven't talked about this."

"No" Nomalisa laughed "but we have been making love and loving expands the world. It'll expand our lives and me too for a while, anyway."

Surprised I blushed "I had not thought about children but I . . . I can be a dad. But how will we fit a child into all we do. A new addition to our family, wow." Later, once I had absorbed Nomalisa's wonderful news I went back to her "A son. I will become a man when I have a son."

We decided to marry at the local courthouse with only a couple of our college friends as witnesses. It was our intention to have a full traditional wedding, with me paying the bride price or lebola, and her family coming from the Transkei to my village once the baby was born. Unfortunately just as we were getting really excited at the prospect of our first boy, Nomalisa had a miscarriage and became deeply depressed. She threw herself into her work. Our wedding celebrations were forgotten, and much of my free time was spent grieving with her. I almost enjoyed our mutual agony and regret. A strange comment I know but when my father died I was protected from the pain and was expected to grow strong and protective without sharing any feelings. Now I was invited to cry with Nomalisa and with the AIDS family who faced tragedy every day. Somehow these experiences together helped me feel more like a citizen of the world and less of a smouldering inhibited child.

Once my training in journalism was complete, I searched assiduously for suitable jobs without success. Finally, with some help from a careers advisor I secured a contract position at a call centre. Now I had more time with Nomalisa, as we were able to coordinate our shifts. While I found the job incredibly boring, I was earning more than I had at the petrol station and used every spare minute I had to improve my writing skills. I also applied for every position that appeared to offer a move towards journalism. I became a volunteer at the AIDS clinic where Nomalisa now had a paid position and life again settled into a routine. Two years after her miscarriage Nomalisa fell pregnant again and had twins, a boy and a girl. Now life became incredibly hectic with me helping out as much as I could so we could both still work.

I continued applying for jobs whenever I found one that seemed to offer a move closer to journalism. This is how I came to apply for and get the work with Cape Town Talks. I was delighted when I got one interview and then another and when I was offered the job I was over the moon. We were sad at my moving to Cape Town but set this aside, invited Nomalisa's mother to move in and help with the twins, and I went out to pursue my fortune.

Nomalisa said as I left "you my man go conquer the world. As soon as you are ready for us I will follow. I love you."

Themba - Getting a grip on politics

I was so excited at having a job related to journalism that I was happy to start at the bottom. But what I had not anticipated was the antagonism around me. The Cape Town Talks team immediately made it clear I was a very poor second to their first choice, a young white woman who had topped her class with a dual major in communications and international development. I was also not prepared for my defensiveness. As I struggled to hold my own in an environment where everyone seemed to want me to fail, I resorted to texting college mates at every opportunity with witty put downs of both staff and callers to the station. This just exacerbated the problem.

However, despite my growing anger and disquiet at CTT I found an insatiable desire growing to truly understand my environment and the politics that drove the discontent of so many people I heard over the airways. With the one hour's train travel each way between home and work I began reading. There was much written about Apartheid and the hardships of all who weren't white. There were many books about the ANC, Mandela and other leaders who worked tenaciously in the struggle to gain power both from within and without South Africa. I was also surprised to learn that the resistance movement included both South Africans and external supporters, as well as people of every colour and creed, including whites. I read copiously, but no book satisfied my desire to understand the huge disparity between the privilege of some and the utter poverty and loss of hope among most South Africans. Also, why were so many people still so unhappy?

What had happened in the past twenty-one years to shatter the hope of the common man? How had the dream for a new democracy with freedom and prosperity for the rainbow nation come to this? Why had our hope that the ANC would take power and govern for all been buried under story upon story of corruption?

Madiba had told our nation in 2000 "Massive poverty and obscene inequality are such terrible scourges of our times . . . they have to rank alongside slavery and Apartheid.

"Overcoming poverty is not a gesture of charity, it is an act of justice. It is the protection of a fundamental human right, the right to dignity and a decent life."

These words stirred something deep inside and I resolved, "I will join the ranks of those who, despite the assault on the whistle blowers of our country, stand against the corruption of the state. I will work to out the kleptocracy that our ANC government has become and help build the dignity of our nation."

At work I try to integrate what I am reading with the voices that continually invite us, as a well-respected mouthpiece of the Western Cape, to make their views known to other South Africans and to our political leaders. How will I find a place to have some impact? I am at the bottom of the food chain, so how and why will I find a true calling as part of CTT? And once I have found my place, what will I do to secure my way up the ladder? I have made a big sacrifice in leaving my family, as have they in letting me come here. I must make this work.

Despite many calls on Xenophobia that day I can't stop thinking about the lady who talked so openly about her Khoi–San ancestors being raped by all comers. She said the government still saw themselves as "the ANC" rather than the South African government. "They plunder our land, support those who dig up and sell our diamonds and gold. They tack shacks together instead of building reasonable houses for the poor while Mr Zuma pours millions into his own mansions. They support those who steal electricity while our lights go out, they spend millions renaming roads instead of building desperately needed infrastructure when for heavens sake people know that Robert Sobukwe Road with its shiny new signs is still the old road to Modderdam.

"And what about the Rhodes statue at UCT? Do they seriously think smearing it in faeces and having it removed can wipe out South African history? I don't think so! But the biggest tragedy is that every day this government steals people's hope and dignity. What was the TRC for . . . Things are worse now than under Apartheid.

"I am a youth worker and in schools I see it every day. In every class I am confronted with kids whose whole family are slaves to alcohol or Tik. Both signs of hopelessness and the violence in Khayelitsha is out of control. What hope do we have while these problems go unchecked? This country is a mess and until we confront these issues and work together we have no hope. God forgive us."

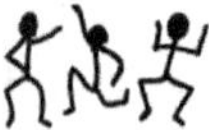

As Nalendi comes off air I begin babbling. "What are Tik and Khayelitsha?"

"Tik is methamphetamine, the drug they call 'ice' overseas, a very destructive drug which seems to be sold everywhere in Khayelitsha which is an huge informal township on the Cape Flats. There everyone lives on top of each other usually in corrugated iron shacks. Crime, that's rape, murder, burglary, street violence, gangs, whatever you can think of, happens there. Khayelitsha is unsafe for everyone whether they are residents or venture in by mistake. Be warned. Don't go there and definitely steer clear after dark."

"Oh I see. Well I was listening to our last caller and we must do more to change what is happening." We talk for a couple of hours, first just the two of us then with others from the team about Xenophobia, and anger and hatred. About the horrors throughout Africa and the atrocities of our history and all the way through this time I keep thinking there must be a way for us to help stem the violence. How can I help?

I ask if I can stay back and do some research into Xenophobia and for the first time Nalendi smiles at me and is supportive. "Sure we pay for the internet anyway, just remember that we have load shedding between 6.30 and 8.30 but I think the café down the road has a wood fired Pizza oven so you could grab dinner there if you stay back that late."

I do stay back a while and google about Xenophobia but leave as load shedding kicks in. I feel so sad. It is good to be part of the team but somehow letting myself enjoy them sets me thinking about how I haven't seen my family for over three months now. How I miss them. I wish I could cuddle close to Nomalisa and let the kids, who couldn't walk when I left, crawl all over me. I phone home and speak for a few minutes but it's not the same. Everyone is doing well and is pleased to hear from me but, aware of the costs, we keep it short. As I sit back I feel tears on my cheeks and brush them away angrily. I still believe a Zulu man does not cry.

My mind wanders back to all the things I have lost. It's taken me so many years to get to this lowly place. I lost my father, my mother was never there, my education was sketchy and now I am the butt of jokes at CTT. I have lots to be angry about, but am I also a perpetrator. That damn caller. I didn't rape her or her people. I owe her nothing.

The next morning I get in early, turn again to Mr Google, type Truth and Reconciliation and find an article stressing that the TRC did not include the 'ordinary' victims of Apartheid. This rings so true. What about those of us who have lost out because of migrant labour, a bad education, removal from our land or even just by watching and doing nothing as Apartheid happened.

I can't wait for Nalendi to have her first break. "Do you know that the TRC only worked with perpetrators of violence and their victims but not with 'ordinary' people who were affected by Apartheid, things like forced removals in the community? Are we are doing enough by saying 'No to Xenophobia' and giving people space to talk?"

Others pitch in and the discussion becomes animated. Each one of us remembers unresolved feelings. For Nalendi there are things she has not thought about for a long time. For Samuel and I, incidents and memories are closer to the surface. Mary's face reddens whenever we speak. "How can I, a white girl, dare to worry about my issues when I am one whose parents voted for Apartheid?"

Now when callers phone in we wonder what is behind their remarks and, prompted by our off air discussions, Nalendi begins to probe gently about the motivations behind callers' remarks. More people phone and Mary and I struggle to deal with all the calls. It's like the fires again. Callers are ringing in by the tens and twenties. Cape Town seems so keen to talk about their feelings. Everyone has an opinion about Xenophobia and, more than that, everyone has a personal story they want to share. There are so many feeling unheard, displaced, desperate, angry and hopeless. Nalendi begins to give out Lifeline's number to people whom she can't contain and off air we buzz with agitated excitement, but also fall over each other with ideas of where to next.

I turn to Mr Google again. Now I am looking for what we can do and where to refer people. And what about our own memories? I typed in memories and healing and find that there is an institute right here in Cape Town that does just that in places like Mitchell's Plain and Khayelitsha exactly the places our callers keep referring to.

I phone the institute and speak to a wonderful lady who seems to know exactly what I am talking about. She slows me down and says perhaps I need to deal with myself first. When I get off the phone I talk to my teammates about going in to meet this lady and they become quite agitated. "Why would you do that shouldn't it be . . . ?" Mary actually interrupts and says "Hey what about us?" and the conversation takes another turn.

After a while I steer the conversation back and suggest inviting the lady to come and talk on air to CTT. This excites everyone so I phone the Institute again and make the arrangements for later that week. It needs to be quick because news never stands still. The interview is fantastic. We are told about a process where people come together to share their stories about difficult and unresolved issues in their lives. How they are led through a process of beginning to let go of the pain, fear and anger that has controlled them so that they can begin to move towards forgiveness. "A number are freed by this process to embark on a gentler path." Callers queue for ages to get through.

Everyone at the station is enthusiastic. My teammates begin to laugh with me and within a couple of days I have forgotten their earlier animosity. Carried on the swell of eagerness coming from callers, we work like Trojans. There is so much to do that we begin to share tasks, working outside of our strict job descriptions, talk to each other continually about what needs to be done and in this process new ideas keep coming.

In our weekly staff meeting I suggest: "What if we organise a Healing of Memories workshop, invite callers to volunteer and then talk about it on air?" The whole team is excited and I, as instigator, am tasked with finding out about costs and possibilities. Nalendi agrees to approach management and to pursue sponsorship if I can make it happen.

Heal your Memories

"You're on Nalendi, One, two, three."

"Good morning all. Today I want to begin with a follow up on an interview we had last week. As you know we have been flooded with calls about your memories of what has happened to you either during the Apartheid era or because of the hang over's of Apartheid. Well we at CTT are wanting to do more than simply talk about South Africa's collective trauma. We want to be part of helping to build in a small way towards a better, more inclusive, future and have found a way to begin.

"We will run a 'Healing of Memories' workshop here in Cape Town and are looking for volunteers. If you listened to our program last week and are interested you can phone in and ask to speak to Themba who will ask you a few questions and get back to you if you are chosen to take part. We will be looking for a mix of people so if you are not selected you can still take part through talkback once the workshop has happened. So please jump in. Our lines will be open first thing each morning this week and we will select four people a day. So remember, Themba is the person to speak to if you are interested. Keep listening because we want everyone to benefit from this initiative either as a participant or as a commentator once we bring what has happened in the project back on air."

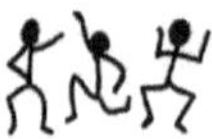

Now my work begins in earnest. As expected, many people call and the selection process is vigorous. I do the initial assessment over the phone. If people meet the broad criteria they are then called back by a professional who assesses their suitability as a participant robust enough to share their stories publicly. Within the week we have twenty participants and two standbys.

Sponsorship comes easily. This project is clearly meant to fly and before I know it I am off with Nalendi to Monkey Valley for our Healing of Memories weekend retreat. I will participate, but Nalendi will only be an observer because as an announcer she does not want to share her experiences publicly.

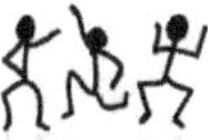

Driving down to Monkey Valley is amazing. After four and a half months I have learned to accommodate to the changing moods of Table Mountain, but I gasp at her beauty as we snake down the peninsula between her spine and the sea. The Twelve Apostles peek out above a subtle shawl of scattered mist, and the Chapman's Peak drive to Noordhoek, carved into the cliffs and dropping one hundred meters into the boiling ocean, is nothing short of spectacular. How, I wonder, are we to 'beware of falling rocks?' Will those flimsy looking fishing nets restrain rock falls? We stop for a moment and look back across from just below the peak to Hout Bay. The sea is a deep aquamarine. The sunshine across the bay and up to Lion's head is half shrouded behind a lace shawl of stratus cloud. I cannot imagine a more stunning sight. And then without words we climb back into the car and drive on.

In Noordhoek we turn off the main road and slow down as we enter a tunnel cut through a milkwood forest and stop beside a simple timber structure snuggled into the bush, leave our belongings in the car and stroll into the building and then out onto the terrace. Another amazing view. The trees are cut away to frame a sandy white beach that stretches to the horizon. Wow! I have never been to the sea before, never walked in the sand along the ocean. How will I resist?

"Are you sure this is our retreat?" I ask as a man approaches us and offers assistance.

"We are the forward party for the CTT workshop. I am Nalendi and this is Themba." We are shown to the facilitator's quarters, a cottage even closer to the beach.

"Please make yourselves at home and let me know when you wish to see the conference area set aside for your use."

We get our things from the car, wander down to our cabin, throw our belongings into our rooms, sit on the balcony and drink a coffee. Then Nalendi heads off to look at the workshop facilities and suggests I head for the beach. "Thanks! I have never been on a beach before."

I wander down a boardwalk through the scrub, scramble between a few rocks and am on the sand. It is breathtaking. I remove my shoes and sand squeaks between my toes, the ocean growls and the wind whispers as I stride towards the water. The foam capped waves hover shimmering against an azure sky. Nothing is still and yet a peace pervades the air. The sun warms my back but I shiver as ribbons of pale, laced foam tickle my toes.

I look up the length of the beach and see small clusters of people waking dogs of all sizes. They stop to say good day and then rush off as their charges chase each other in and out of the waves.

A blur flashes into sight, hooves thud, sand is swept up and water churns as five thundering horses race the full length of the beach. I smile as horsetails and manes flash past flagging their delight at freedom. This is magic, plucked from a fairy tale. I take out my cell phone and click madly as I try to capture this enchantment for posterity. How will I get anyone to share my delight and how will I hold onto this wonder in times to come?

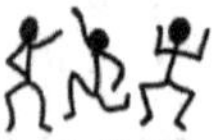

The ambiance in the dining area is subdued. The thatched roof and dark timber walls absorb sound and the generous glass windows draw in the rumble of ocean and purple gold of sunset. A cluster of people chat animatedly around the fire and a lone man stares out to sea. I enter, smile, raise my hand in greeting and wander over to the window. "Hi, I'm Themba, fantastic view!" "Sam," "Ah the fisherman. Have you just arrived?" He blushes. "No, been here a while. I recognise that deep baritone. I spoke to you on the phone. I like to be early." We chat about the day's catch and the magic of our surroundings until we are invited to join the others for a meal. Crusty bread and delicious chowder followed by a wonderful sticky pudding. By the end of dinner, people are settled and ready to work.

Our weekend facilitator stands "Hi my name for those of you to whom I have not introduced myself is Simon. Please follow me, we will reconvene in our workspace." We stand and follow.

There are twenty-six of us who move into a circle in a spacious work area alongside the dining room. Again the view! How will I ever concentrate on the work at hand? That sea and the stars. I could almost stretch out my hand and grab one.

A woman speaks and I turn to listen. "I'll find it hard to concentrate in this spell-binding place! OK. Alison. Breathe in, and allow yourself to settle. I will take responsibility for your attention. Now I know that some of you have travelled far today and that traffic was bad. Are you all comfortable? . . . Have you found your rooms? . . . Do you have a welcome pack? . . . If not see Geoff. Stand up Geoff. . . OK it's taken us a while to get here and we have a way to go together.

"As you know this is a special program put together by CTT but it draws on learnings from the Healing of Memories program. Each facilitator is a volunteer who can offer support and listen, and we believe this workshop is important. Now I will hand over to Nalendi who all of you know."

"Hi and welcome everyone! We are very excited about this project. As you know we are building on the idea that all South Africans need healing and we take from the TRC the fundamental principle that 'to forgive is not just to be altruistic, [but] it is the best form of self-interest', and that sharing difficult experiences with sympathetic others helps us deal with trauma.

"Now a couple of rules. People have each signed an agreement to maintain the confidentiality of others and share only their own story on radio. You also understand that I will make no personal disclosures, but will be here for the whole workshop and will spend some time with each group. No one is to speak for another either within or outside this forum. We would like you to keep phones off during sessions and please wear your nametag at all times. OK guys and girls lets have fun, and thank you for being part of this bold experiment."

Alison now stands and says that each of us has been assigned to a group of five and that much of our work will happen with these people. She then asks each of us to share with the person next to us who we are and why we have decided to come. I turn and am off. While I have asked each participant questions over the phone, I haven't shared my dream. I want to talk about the continual nagging pain. I am terrified that everyone I love will leave me.

After introducing our partner to the group, we watch aghast as Alison bursts into tears and tells us how she saw her brother dragged away by the police. She then looks up, smiles and asked us to reflect on what moved us, what we were feeling and what we related to. "Were any memories triggered?"

We sit awhile and then take a ten minute break. After the break, we move into the small groups we have been assigned to and discuss our feelings. Once we have talked in our group we take our leave and go to bed.

Healing Group

Next morning we start early, have breakfast and break into groups. Alison begins by saying that we will spend a lot of today and some of tomorrow together. "And as you can see I won't say a word man." She laughs.

Our first exercise is to draw a timeline of our lives and mark significant events along the way. Then we are asked who would like to begin first. The stories will be recorded for later transcription so that Nalendi can refer to them if she wants to work on background for her radio programs. "No personal story or part thereof will be repeated outside of this room except by the storyteller."

Soda is a smiling, spritely, ageless man with the most beautiful weathered face and a full but gap toothed smile. His expression changes with each utterance.

It's hard to know where to begin. I have seen many things, faced many disappointments and felt great sadness but it is not like me to fear or get angry. I rather try to get even and most often I do this without getting into trouble although you can see that I'm half Hottentot and that's bad here whatever government is in power.

We have lived in the Bo-Kaap for many generations. I am lucky hey. I lived there all my life but many others were removed. We lived together with other families in the same house. At one time there were us Muslims, Chinese, a Jew and Indians all in the same block. You know this old black woman cared for us because my mother worked and then when I had children I took them to her. She said no I'm too old but then she called me a skelm and grew my children up. We'd wash in the same bathroom and eat from the same pot but when we went out there was a bench for blacks and coloureds and another one for whites and you know there were lots of toilets for whites and none for blacks so we had to piss on the side of the road. And then they would think we were dirty when we smelled like we pooped our pants. What did they expect man.

But it never affected me. You know I would go swimming in the city baths and on white beaches. Man I was whiter than many of them tanned ones. This one time when I was young this guy took my money for a ticket at the door on the way in then came and got me out of the pool and said that I would get him in trouble because I was clearly non-white. I was little but I argued man and said but you sold me a ticket. I was loud so he said OK. Who was going to see me anyway we were there to swim not look at what colour we were.

And this time we had been swimming at Green Point beach and we were waiting for a bus. We waited for an hour man and all these white busses came by and none for us so I left my sisters and jumped on a white bus. Nothing happened man, except that they got home two hours later and told my mother.

It was a good life. We had no shoes but we went to a mixed school and we all learned the same things. Then the blacks were removed and I lost my best friend. Years later I was hanging out with some friends and we got into an argument with these black guys and I was teasing this guy and he told me I was a stupid Griqua and I was cheeky with him and then suddenly I recognised him. I asked him where he came from and why he was in Bo-Kaap. He said he used to live here and then I knew. It was my friend from school and I was hugging him and the others asked what I was doing we were supposed to be fighting but I said no man this was my special friend from school and we just went off together. Now we visit man. I go to his house even though it is far away and he comes to me and we are still friends. It is special man just like in the old days.

And even now man when I wander around Bo-Kaap I hang out with other people man. There is this Somali who has a shop near the Mosque and I hang out there as if it's my own. If it's hot I take the liberty man and just say come into my office and he smiles and listens while we talk. It's my special brand of Griqua chutzpah. I do that everywhere man because they all know me in this place.

You know now that my parents are gone and we have been left three houses in Bo-Kaap between seven of us and it is a problem because we have to divide these houses between us but how can we do it because if I want to sell one house then where will I live and the same for my sisters and Mr Smarty-pants my youngest brother who wants to sell and live by the sea, so we are stuck here man. You see Bo-Kaap is changing, it's getting 'gentrified' yong (he laughs), but we are here for good man. It's where we come form.

This is the place where my kids were born and where my son died man. It's the only place I know so how ever upper class the place gets man I will remember what I had. I will remember not being good enough because I was black and now I'm not good enough because I'm a Hottentot but I will do what I want just you wait and see they are not throwing me out because I don't match their décor man. I'm here till they take me to that Mosque on the corner near the Somali shop. They will carry me out feet first. Even if I bring down the prices of their spivvy places full of fancy shit. I don't care. This is my Bo-Kaap and I will live here as long as the South Wester blows. It is the spirit of my forefathers that lives there. It will always be because they can drive people out but they can't make it safe. The skollies roam the streets and steal from the rich but they know me and they smile and say hi Soda whenever they see me and then they move on. Sometimes I join them man but now I'm a bit old and I can't run so good. He smiles. Just kidding man. What more do you want to know? But seriously watch out for skollies when you go there. It's not safe man. People are starving today so they steal to eat. When Apartheid was here it was colour that was the problem now it's colour and hunger man. Lots of people go hungry. I'm lucky I have friends and family but if you don't have that in Cape Town you're in trouble.

Soda's face distorts and he fights tears. His story is told and he is spent. Someone takes his hand and we sit in silence.

"Thank you Soda. Would anyone like to comment?"

"Fantastic sense of humour dude. Sorry about your son. Did he die a long time ago?"

"Better to stick with comments rather than questions."

"No man that's fine. He died twelve years ago but no man should bury a child and it hurts like it happened yesterday."

The silence deepens. After several minutes Alison asked is anyone else ready to speak. People were still quiet a while and then Linda speaks.

"OK I will have a go."

She looks at her timeline and sighs.

I was born into Apartheid, grew up in District Six but had no awareness until about seven.

I had a White mum, Asian dad and lived a happy well-balanced family life with four brothers and three sisters. Everyone else thought the District was poverty-stricken but for me life was just about having a family.

Mum's adopted sister lived with us, and a friend of hers, Aunty Dolly, worked in Camps Bay. My aunt and I visited Aunt Dolly who was the housekeeper and she lived in the garden cottage. Her employers lived in a beautiful house and I often played with their daughter who was my age.

This little girl wore a matching nighty, gown and slippers and I remember thinking is this what being rich is? Living in a house in Camps Bay with matching sleep wear and slippers. I had an enjoyable time but this was the first time I noticed what people have and don't.

As I grew older I would accompany my dad whenever he went out. He used to fish at Oudekraal. I can remember when we went on the busses Mum could sit downstairs and Dad and I upstairs. Whenever we went out Dad was so outspoken about politics. Dad was a friend of Jimmy La Guma the communist who lived in Roger Street in District Six and the two of them often got into heated arguments about the Apartheid policies.

I don't like confrontations and I was scared that my dad would get into trouble with the law and I worried how we would face life without a father. I didn't like the feelings so at thirteen I stopped going out with my dad.

Themba sighs. He certainly knew what it was like to live life without a father. He turns away from Linda and wipes his eyes. This is her story but he feels with her or perhaps for himself. It is hard to forgive and forget. Perhaps this process just opens old wounds. He will have to guard against his hurt coming out.

I first became fully aware of Apartheid when I began work. As Coloureds we were paid less than White employees and had to use separate toilets and staff rooms. In the beginning it was not so bad. I was a clerk in a linen company owned by Whites but then I got a job at Truworths on the Foreshore, Cape Town. Here one would not get a job if you had a 'kroes kop' or were too dark. You also had to have a good figure. You were chosen because of your looks and if you were a 'fair complexioned' Coloured person.

Often the bosses of other companies would try to seduce you and if you wanted a promotion you were well advised to comply. Women would keep quiet about these things to preserve their jobs.

Truworths stores sold high fashion ladies clothes and the store was close to Cape Town Docks where visitors from ocean liners, sailors and foreigners often shopped. There were two Coloured sales clerks, a lady from Woodstock who was the bookkeeper, a German Jewish shoe sales woman, an Afrikaner and an Italian and of course the tea girl was dark. There was also an English window-dresser and one Muslim and one Christian seamstress.

A Swiss lady came to work with us. I was to call her Mrs and she could call me Linda. She had to learn to speak Afrikaans and I had to teach her my job. One day we happened to see each other's pay slips. I had earned R45 and she got R80. She was shocked. 'Linda why do I get more than you? I am sure this is wrong. I will take this matter up with to the manageress.' I replied 'if you do that we will both be fired.' She was very interested in this.

Another effect of Apartheid was that I had to live in an overcrowded home with my parents, and my friend could live where she wanted. She had a flat in Tamboerskloof and invited me. I was her tour guide and we became firm friends.

In 1971 my dad died and we had been evicted to the Cape Flats through the Group Areas Act and lived in Hanover Park. When my friend saw where I lived she couldn't believe the distance I had to travel to work. At first our new semi-detached maisonette was quite nice but soon our area became a rundown horrible place. I remember we arrived there on 15 of December and knew no one. Groups of gangs evolved very quickly due to forced removals from 42 areas and soon the community life changed when these gangs disrupted the lives of people.

I grew up with gangsters in District Six and they did not target children whereas the gangsters in the townships had no ambition and they targeted children. In District Six every child had to attend school however poor they were. With displacements mother's also had to work and there were no schools in the townships. The children became latchkey kids. Left at home alone, when kids went outside of their homes gangsters made them feel like they belonged and then trained them to break into other people's houses or sell drugs. To become a gang member you had to do break ins, rape and even murder as initiation.

The problems today with drugs, drug addicts and drug lords came when close-knit communities were uprooted and people needed to re-establish themselves. People had to live with and adapt to these atrocities.

This story certainly gets under my skin. I joined a gang because I was alone, homeless and without hope. I bite my lip and refocus on Linda.

It was horrible. I felt degraded, angry, afraid, traumatised and much poorer. We had to find bus and train fares and had no social lives after daylight hours.

We loved the mountains and the sea and had to give up both because travel became too dangerous.

In the words of Ronnie Cloete of De Korte Street "In District Six living was cheap and life precious. Now in Hanover Park living is expensive and life is cheap." (This message is taken from an embroidered memory cloth in the District Six museum.)

My younger son went to a model C school, which took Coloureds who could afford to pay for their education. He went to school in the northern suburbs and was my youngest child. One day he wanted to invite two kids home and I asked what their names were. I wanted to find out their racial classification. One was a Muslim and the other a black kid. He said why are you asking such a stupid question and I realised that he was totally unaware of Apartheid. I on the other hand was conditioned by the system and I realised that it was not politically correct to mention the word 'race'.

I also remember an incident that happened to my eldest son who is now forty. We used to go camping and on one occasion in Hartenbos near Mossel Bay, he went in and asked for a haircut. The barber told my son that he had ethnic hair, which he could not cut. He spoke as if it were the texture that made it difficult to cut but it was clearly his prejudice against Non-Whites and his incompetence to cut all kinds hair.

In the past Coloureds were very caught up in concerns that our people may bring their "family down because their kids look different." Now education is an important divider, as is where you live. We are always asking, "where are your people from."

I used to be very insecure. I lacked confidence, didn't feel valued in the workplace because of the way I was addressed. I was never given my rightful title but was always only Linda. I earned less and never had the chance to stand up for myself because of fear of losing my job so I would swallow my tears because I couldn't stand up.

There are moments when things still come up but now I cope with it by confronting the issue and saying how I feel with confidence.

I have done many interviews, researched and worked at the District Six museum for ten years, from 1994 to 2004. It was an organic process. I worked as an Education Officer and have done tons of school programs and walking tours into District. You name it, I have done it.

I know I helped people cope with their suffering by listening to their stories.

Does it help I wonder. I'm not feeling so good listening to you. In fact I'm quite wound up.

When we left District Six I felt that I had lost my identity, we lost our identities. We were displaced, I felt like a 2nd class citizen. The Whites ruled and it was all about "White supremacy." The community was taken away in trucks and no one asked us how we felt.

After 1994, the Truth and Reconciliation process was put in place, now there is counselling for everybody and everything. We didn't have therapy then. We believed we would be arrested if we talked. At the time of the forced removals we did not even realise that we had such a thing as 'human rights.' We had to obey the law during the Apartheid era. From 1994 we slowly started to gain the confidence to talk openly.

The director of the museum, Sandy Prosalendis played a major role during my time at the District Six museum. I had so much to learn about our past history, which was kept from us. I admire and have great respect for her. She believed in me more than I believed in myself. She was my mentor and I love her dearly.

My healing process came with seeing "District Six: The Musical" by Taliep Petersen and David Kramer. I had been working at a company in the 1980's and a White man raved about this play and said, "You must go." He enjoyed it so much.

Since I left the area in 1971 I never put foot there again. If people asked me where I had lived I said in Cape Town and left it at that. When I saw a familiar face we would chat about where we lived with nostalgia and sadness and now having to travel by train for one and a half hours to get anywhere. When I felt any twinge of loss I would push it down.

Two weeks before the end of the season at the Baxter I decided that I must go and see "District Six: The Musical." I took my family to see the show. In the foyer we saw people from the old neighbourhood. We had lost contact with them during the forced removals. Seeing them was wonderful and sad. Then we sat in the auditorium and the play began to unfold before us. It was funny and sad. It was my life. It was dark in the theatre so no one could see that I was soaked with tears. It was so painful to acknowledge that this had happened to us. After the show I couldn't sleep, couldn't talk to anyone and then I began to write my autobiography. It was not written in anger but I didn't hide anything.

This was my turning point, acknowledging what had happened. I did not want to admit it. I had cut off my memories and battled inwardly for years. At that point I decided that I would not carry the baggage of Apartheid on my shoulders any longer. I was only hurting myself and I wanted to move forward with my life.

My brother and dad were always full of anger and this was not healthy. They found it hard to come to terms with the past and their suffering through Apartheid and the injustices that they were forced to live with. These issues contributed to their early passing away.

"I remember that musical. "My Broertjie My Bra". I used to sing that all the time. It was sort of like a symbol of resistance. But you never really forget do you? And District six is a symbol still. I wonder if people will ever build there or will it be a scar on the face of Cape Town forever. Will you forget?"

"No not forget but I have put the pain in perspective . . . I . . ."

"Thanks for that story it brings back so much for me" says Warren "I'm sorry about your dad and your brother. It's so sad . . ."

"OK people we have done well this morning. Lets take a tea break and then another session before we have lunch, then another session and maybe a walk on the beach. Is everyone ready to leave what we have heard in the group? And remember, everyone here and in the other groups have been talking about painful stuff. Go gently with each other."

We nod and slowly drift into the meals area. All ravenous we head for the scones. This is heavy work and we need refuelling.

I laugh with a couple of people about being looked after and then someone from another group begins to talk about the news and my job at CTT and I move away. I'm not in the mood for this. Can't he see I'm not all here? I'm thinking about my dad and about Sizani. I haven't seen her for such ages. Apartheid ruined my life. Those damn Boers stole my father and my mother and . . . I move onto the deck and wipe angry tears from my eyes. "Why am I here? This is a waste of time. O hell . . ."

Nalendi comes up to me and touches my arm. "Hang in there, Themba. It's hard on us all but I think it's worth it." I stare out to sea. I could just run for the beach and walk for miles. I smile and turn to join my group and we wander back to our workroom together.

More Evictions

Soda is laughing. "Hey you guys Chill. Life's OK man! You just got to laugh at history. Don't let it get to you. You always win if you can just laugh."

"OK Soda its time to get back to work now. Who wants to go next?"

"I will," says Warren.

Family and roots are very important to me and that's why I've researched my family history. To know who is my family? Where I'm from? How I tie in with society? To leave a legacy of this history to my family.

Four generations ago my great, great, great grandfather arrived in South Africa, we believe on a slave ship. It was spotted by a British Patrol and he was among the human cargo jettisoned at sea during a police raid just off Simon's Town. The owners would be fined and their ship forfeited if the British caught them with slaves on board. Lucky he could swim . . . . Simon's town was a British naval base and belonged to them until 1957.

We know the slaves were named after the towns they came from but are not sure if he came from India from a place called Kindu, or from the Congo where there is a Mount Kibu.

What we do know is that Reverend Bernard Shaw, a Methodist minister, took him in and gave him a piece of land between the manse and the church to farm, and that he planted tea. Tea was grown in Kindu. I like spicy Indian food and eastern custom and if I were to go anywhere I'd go east not west. My father was like me, and so black that if you took a photo of him it would come out blue. My father's brother Michael also searched and believes that there's also a link to the Congo.

My great, great, great grandfather married a Levendall and lived in Red Hill a short while and then built or bought a house in Runsman's Drive, Simon's Town. Later he moved to where Cardiff Road hits the mountainside where my grandfather and my father were born. My grandmother lived in this three-story rock house, against the mountain, next a waterfall and with a view of the sea.

I spent a lot of time in that house.

Ya! You know I never knew what it was like to have my clothes cleaned, or to fish because if I wanted fish I'd go to the harbour and say uncle and he would say yes take a fish and take one for your mommy as well; or to buy oranges or guavas because my grandmother had guava and orange trees.

My mother worked at Solute cleaners and the fisherman, who always called her Aunty Ivy even though they were the same age, would ask, "will you clean my pants" and she'd say sure. An hour later they'd be clean and he'd say, "I owe you." Then over the weekend he'd knock on the door and say "here's a bunch of fish.'

I grew up with baboons. They were dangerous but we knew our way around them. We played on the mountainside with them as children. Playing cowboys and crooks, building swings amongst them. It surprises me that they are now considered a nuisance. They were in the trees or on the roofs at grandma's, so amongst us all the time. We fed them, sharing with them as they shared with us. They didn't destroy or fight and never came into our houses. Even the dogs knew to accept them. There was a hidden language between the baboons and us. They wouldn't allow us close when they had young, throwing stones at us.

There were some tensions in those times. For instance I met a white girl who also lived in Cardiff Road. As we walked home after school we'd show each other what we'd been doing in our separate schools. But one day my father came to me at night and said, "you mustn't walk around with that child" because her dad had complained to mine. I was in primary school at the time.

Soda interrupts. "All our parents were scared hey! My Ma . . . "

"Soda please! Warren needs us to listen. Can we focus on his timeline please?"

We'd play up to the caretaker asking to hit a little on the local tennis court knowing we weren't allowed because of our colour so we got him back. We would walk along the road above the courts on our way home from school and throw stones down so that whoever wanted to play tennis would first need to clean the court.

My father was a bus driver, and there were some very painful experiences on the busses. The first three rows were reserved for 'whites only,' the rest was for coloureds. That made me very sad was when I saw an older person standing with empty seats in front when my father was driving. He had no power to say, "old lady you can sit down" even with no one sitting there, because the whites would protest. The bus would also pass us with a 'whites only' sign with us standing in the rain with my dad driving. These things made me sad but over all I remember a happy life with close connections to family and community.

And then came the Group Areas Act. It affected us all.

At first we were told by Simon's Town Councillor Reilly that the defence area was to be extended right up to Glen Carne and civilians were to be removed in case of attack. Many people accepted that. Others knew it was a 'White lie.'

When forcibly removed the fishermen were told they could launch out in Noordhoek and Kommetjie but it didn't materialise and life was never the same for them.

I sigh deeply and move over to the window. Linda comes and stands next to me. "It's hard to listen to isn't it?"

"Sure is!"

"Sorry Warren. You two rejoin us please."

"I can't listen to this. It's the same over and over. Why did we let it go on for so long?"

"I know you're finding this hard but can you join us please."

"Bugger this. I don't want to know! Its over man." I storm out of the room but when no one follows I slow myself down and then go back in.

"Ready to listen?"

"Sorry man! I think so." Lucky I'm black because my cheeks are burning. I am so embarrassed. I'm supposed to be helping here. But I'm so angry, so sad so . . .

My grandmother who had lived in a three-story house against the mountain overlooking all of False Bay was put into a single room flat in Ocean View with my father's sister who was a spinster on the ground floor supposedly because of her age. Fenced in with one gate for the whole area so that people's comings and goings could be controlled. Both my grandmother and her sister didn't last long out there.

"You mean they died?"

"*Yes they died . . . Our house in Simon's Town was pulled down when the Group Areas Act hit us but my family were humble people, who accepted things and moved on; but we were deeply affected.*"

"We all were!"

The only place that stood firm and strong was Kalk Bay. Everyone refused to move. The coloured people, trawler owners and fishermen, and the whites in the area all refused.

Then you could still relate people to place. Kindo, Jacobs and Emmanuel's came from Simon's Town. Kindo's came from Simon's Town or Heathfield and if they had money Grassy Park. People with no money like my dad, you went to Ocean View. Back then people related to the surnames.

Ocean View was set up for the people from Simon's Town with no consideration given to the children who were moved at all. In Simon's Town we lived in big houses with room for many. In Ocean View houses were small with no thought for growing families. So if two or three children needed housing, families were splintered. Like us, we went to Mitchell's Plain for about eighteen years and then I bought a house in Mandalay.

When Mandela was released many things changed and Uncle Bill and I started following up on getting our property back. We were fortunate. I started looking around with the hope of coming back home to my roots.

I looked in Ocean View because I couldn't afford Simon's Town but my cousin is a builder so he bought us out agreeing to keep the house in the family. It's called Kindo Villa and funnily enough my uncle Bill is now called Villa. If you go up Cardiff Road you will see it. I have given all the stuff my grandmother left in my trust to him because I know he will look after it. The organ we played, books that my great, great grandfather signed have all gone to him and his house has become the third museum in Simon's Town.

The other two are the Anglican Church museum with a small Kindo section in a corner, and Amlay's house, which still stands close to the yacht club. But Amlay's house is a more meaningful museum because it has people who are in touch with, and can tell their history. I will pass on any information I glean to Amlay because she can relate things to people.

I still go to the barber in Simon's Town. Lots of us from the old days come here to talk, shout and swear across the shop. A men's gossip collective, where the men chat and the barber Icky says sit still so I can cut. There's a wonderful rapport and I love to go.

There was a time when I couldn't help crying as I drove into Simon's Town but I have overcome that now. Once when I showed my younger son Carl around I caught him crying. He could feel what I was feeling.

I was angry, but now I'm sad because my memories are disconnected. I can't point to the school I went to. It's been taken over by the Navy. The places where we used to play cowboys and crooks have changed. I can't say, 'that was the cannon I used to sit on waiting for my dad.' I have lost my history. When I go to Simon's Town now I have to dig in my memory and try to reshuffle where things were, like the busses turned around at Jubilee Square, the Criterion cinema is now a café. Our house in Dido Valley is still there. But when I went to look, someone came out and asked 'why are you looking at our house?' I said I used to live here. My heart bled as I turned away. I longed to go in but didn't ask because he'd already approached me suspiciously.

I attended a high school in Simon's Town, Arsenal Road Secondary School, and had just started standard eight, a crucial part of my schooling in 1969 or '70. I was head prefect in the final year we went to that school when we were told 'you will have to move.'

There'd always been three streams to Education, the white, black and coloured and we as coloureds got very little support. So for two to three months we had to move ourselves supplying the labour as students. We even carried the furniture.

In our new school in Ocean View we were promised woodwork rooms and a huge soccer field and thought the government was wonderful, but got there to find no lawn. Today the lawn is still all weeds.

My schooling ended there at the end of grade ten.

I was offered an apprenticeship as a carpenter and joiner in the Navel Dockyards and left. I was interested in the electrical field but this was reserved for 'whites' so I did joinery for one year. When the electrical field was partially opened to coloureds a year later I changed but wasn't allowed to do either radio or electronics because these were still restricted. I qualified in the dockyard as a heavy current electrician.

"How lucky are you to have had that opportunity" I mutter to myself "some of us had no chances."

"Do you have something to ask Warren, Themba?"

"Uh . . . Oh no, sorry not really."

"Sorry Warren. Please continue."

I joined the navy and was assigned to work on minesweepers. The Johannesburg, the flagship, was reserved for coloureds. The other six were for whites.

I was the first non-white electrician and they gave me hell. They would make excuses to avoid going to sea and I'd go from ship to ship on a bosun's chair no matter how stormy the sea because each ship needed an electrician on board. I often found myself responsible for maintaining two or three ships while they were at sea. At that time we had no submarines, all the minesweepers were built of wood and not the best in rough weather. In this work I was affected by Apartheid.

Apartheid began when I was in primary school. The English in Simon's Town had behaved badly before the Nationalist Government came in, so we believed in Apartheid. The government gave every child a penny with Verwoerd's face on it and we were all pro-government. To me, as a child, the government was great. We had always heard what the English had been up to and dad was a humble man who accepted and said, 'Yes master, no master.'

Also when Apartheid came in it was hard to tell people apart. We had the choice to either go white or coloured. Within the same family some people were white skinned and their brothers and sisters might be darker.

"Shit this stuff is hard to hear!"

There were three distinct phases of difficulties I faced with Apartheid. Firstly my education was affectively sidelined, then I was limited and bullied in my work in the Navy and thirdly as a teacher.

My first teaching job was at Athlone Technical College, a top college with one of the best results in South Africa but we were in prefab buildings. I began teaching there in 1977. Once again there was the white coloured thing. What hit me most there was the salary. I'd already taken a drop from being a qualified electrician. My white colleagues with the same qualifications got extra, danger money for coming into a coloured area and extra for teaching coloureds. They earned around four times our salary, boasted about it and there was nothing we could do.

"Were you angry?"

No what use is anger? I've learned to do something about it. It is senseless just being angry. I linked up with a number of anti government organisations. I was an executive member of the Public Servants League. We had many near misses of being arrested but linked up with guys like Franklinton and fought Apartheid from an educational perspective.

We had many meetings with the department and made very little headway but I wasn't the kind of guy who would sit in the corner and be angry for the rest of my life. It made me a better person. One of my colleagues moved into law and is very active in areas of inequality now. There are so many who became psychologists, lawyers, doctors in reaction against Apartheid which was good. We were forced to do something positive that we wouldn't have done under normal circumstances. In my case teaching became my life. I am at home in a classroom.

Today when I don't teach, I mentor other teachers and instructors and I challenge them saying "we used to use encyclopaedias. Can you spell encyclopaedia? Now you go to YouTube and things just jump out at you and the class will do it on their own.

What hurt me most under Apartheid were experiences like my father's powerlessness against the system. He drove the bus but the law stopped him supporting his people as driver. There was just nothing he could do.

Warren's voice catches and Linda sighs. I put my ore in "at least you had your father with you. Mine died. At least your family was together. You never had to grow up without a dad."

Warren turns to me with a gentle voice "that's true Themba but you need . . ."

Alison interrupts "please Themba this is not a competition . . . Maybe we can have a chat in the break or if you want to speak to a guy, we have John."

"Sorry Warren! I don't seem to be able to hold this stuff in, but I'm OK Alison. I'll try and keep quiet. Just give me a kick if I interrupt again. Please go on Warren."

That's OK. If I were to hit back I'd say 'if a white person my age didn't make it he must really have been hopeless. Everything around them was designed to help just them.'

Now the blacks are doing what the whites did. We are always caught in the middle.

"Hey man I'm black."

Well I worked under a black guy who was great but then I got two black, female managers. Unreal. Both had chips on their shoulders. They clearly thought, "I'm a black female and I'm going to show you." They'd no understanding that I've faced what they're going through now. If you are black and female now you're away: Confident or not, if you've got a qualification or not, even if you can't do it, you'll get the job.

However, I do have some empathy. After all education is my heartbeat. If you think in terms of a white child that couldn't make it, that child would go to what's called a remedial class. If a coloured child couldn't make it at school they'd go to an adaptation class. That class was normally at the back of the school so that no one could see that there were stupid children at this school. For the blacks there was nothing. So a black child was only allowed to fail twice before he was told to go to work. With that in mind I give a bit.

Most of my students are black and I try and coach them. Many phone me for assistance. If they do phone and are talking fast I have to say 'slow down, talk slower' and they now realise that I am trying to help.

Warren looks over at me.

"Some of you guys had it tough. Some ask me to be their mentor and call me Tata. And I know when they ask me to drop them on top of a bridge and say 'no I'm living under this bridge' that they have a contract for two years and are sending their money home. I have a soft spot for them. Some are basically children, parenting their parents. They share these things with me. It is rewarding when they qualify at the end of the day as electricians and are able to support their families.

But like the lepers, it's only now and again that one comes back to say thanks.

If you are entering the education field for money you should stop, without passion it's too hard.

"Warren I'm afraid our time is up. We need to go in to lunch. Is there anyone with a burning need to speak . . . Warren can you leave it there?"

"Sorry I went over time."

"Not at all. You've experienced much in life. Is everyone ready for lunch? This is exhausting work and we have another session after lunch but then a break and a walk on the beach perhaps. Shall we join the others?"

Memories like water

I choose a table by the window. Exhausted, I want time out. I thought I was tough but the past few months have proved me wrong and now I feel as if I'm drowning in pain and anger. Oh well, no more contemplation. Here they come. The table is set for eight and each space fills.

"Hi, I'm Sean. Do you mind if I join you. I can't get my stuff out of my head. You must have a program on the fishing quotas. It's your ANC boetties man . . . Do you know about it. All our boats are idle because the fishermen can't get licences to go fishing. I used to fish for myself. Had my own boat. Now I have to work for them, they know nothing about the sea but they still rake in the cash and I've lost my boat, work from morning to night no matter the weather and can't get enough to feed my family. They don't even care about our safety. They just want to trawl the sea empty of fish, the bastard ANC. They are worse than the Boers."

"Hey slow down man are you talking about the fishing quotas?"

"Ya it's almost impossible. People put in the papers but they don't get permission. That's why we're selling our boats. It's this government. They don't want anyone except themselves to fish. They keep it all. They are on top and no one else gets a go."

"I've been a fisherman all my life. I left school after grade three and went to fish like my pa and his pa before him. "It's always been hard but now it's almost impossible to get work of any kind. There are so many people going hungry because they can't find a job. If only the government could help people. Give them something to do, clean windows, sweep the streets, earn their own way, but they don't care if people starve. And then when people steal they are surprised and get angry. What are we to do?"

Ahmed looks up from his plate. "Before Apartheid it was easier. Back then there was school for everyone. We had no food or trousers and went to school bare foot but we got an education. For Coloureds, Ya, but it was better than Bantu Education so they said."

I couldn't let that go. "I got my education during the changeover. It was bad before and bad after, unless someone paid for you of course. Now school is bad for everyone unless you can pay. "

I hold my head in my hands for a moment and tune out. This is all too hard. Not even lunch time to myself. I feel like my head will split in two and yet this is my gig man. I rub my eyes and try to pull myself back to the present. I so wish I could just get out of here and sit on the sand. "Nomalisa, you would mange this without thinking but I feel like I'm going Mad."

Ahmed has not noticed my disappearance, he simply smiles and keeps going. "We couldn't go where we wanted but now everything is open. It was easier to get work back then, the money was little . . . but you could buy lots. R10 was like R100 now. And the way the Whites moved us, back then, the Blacks do the same now. Just look. They promised us houses but what do we get? And there was crime but not like now with gangsterism, fighting and killing. It's bad and the Blacks bring in drugs and problems. Oh sorry, Themba, but it's true man. There's a lot of territorial fighting and because our kids are not in school they see it all. Also the gangsters take our kids and teach them how do to do break-ins and smoking and drugs, and before we know it they are traumatised and gangsters themselves."

"I grew up like that. I was in prison for nine years for robbery and hit and run. Got out thirteen years ago. Prison is not for me man." Ahmed looks across the table as others move back in their seats and smiles. "Scared of me? Don't be. I've got work now. But in prison you stay locked up in one room, people take advantage of you and you have to depend totally on yourself. Lucky I had God on my side. He provides, sustains and will always be there." He looks directly into my eyes and says, "Believe in yourself and have faith. You can do anything so long as you have faith. Life isn't hard, you make it hard for yourself. You must believe. You are a Christian, Themba, and I am a Muslim but it makes no difference. God is one. Believe in Him.

"I have four kids of my own and four I adopted. Two three month olds I found in hospital. The others are twelve and nine. Two are in high school and two in year seven. All are from different mothers and each is a gift from God."

Now everyone falls silent. You can hear chewing and someone coughs. I turn to Sean "you were talking man."

Sean smiles "I have faith but sometimes it's difficult. So many young people with no work and nothing to do except run on the streets, form gangs and kill each other. Now in Athlone they have guns. It is very frightening. They fight and even kill each other. Just the other day someone was shot in our street. We're scared, don't know what to do and the government takes no responsibility. They won't help. You should see. They promised houses but there are so many people just sleeping in sacks or sheltering under pieces of iron. They have nowhere to live and nothing to eat, nothing to live for really. But the government behaves in parliament just like children. They grab everything for themselves. Zuma spent millions on a house that he won't pay for. They should tear it down. It is a disgrace. He cares for no one but himself."

"I'm black Sean, but I'm not the ANC man."

"Well my life is hard, harder than it has ever been. Bread goes up by a rand but the pension by only fifty cents. I can't get much work because of the quota system so we're just going backwards."

"Who is we?"

"My beautiful family. My wife works, my oldest daughter lives with us with her two children, eight and five, and I have two boys. One is working and the other one is sixteen and is in school. He plays pool very well and wins competitions. This year he will go overseas to play. Maybe he will go to university but I don't know where the money will come from. I have a good family but it is hard to hope when this government gives us no plan for the future."

"So who will you vote for?"

"Voting means nothing when the government takes everything for themselves. I vote for the DA but the government doesn't care what they say either. Nothing happens here, everything goes backwards."

"You sound hopeless man."

"That's right. My back is bad and I need an operation. I had a disk replaced many years ago. A good doctor did the operation and it healed completely, but then I had to go back to work too soon and it went again. This time the operation didn't work so well and now I'm in constant pain because my vertebrae rub against each other. And my doctor can't operate because I cannot get on the list. So I will have to stop work completely. That's why there's no hope."

I try to swallow my last mouthful. Others sit also stunned into silence. What about confidentiality? We've all been talking about ourselves, and I need a break from this stuff. I guess they're choosing to speak to each other. I'm not used to this personal stuff, it's exhausting and I thought it would be easy. I push my chair back and get up. "We're due back in group in a few minutes. Go grab some desert. I think I'll just grab some fresh air."

 I step out the door and Sara comes up to me. She is in her early twenties and quite lovely. "Hi Sara"

"Hi I was just listening to those guys. Why is it so hard? I was out of work for ages even with my teacher's degree and now I have work but I don't earn enough to live on, never mind enough to save for my dreams. It's not fair. The government is stealing from us and . . ."

"Sorry Sara. It is tough for me too, but now I need to take a breather before we go in again. Please excuse me." I turn and walk off.

Back to the treadmill

"Here we are again. Did everyone have a good lunch? Hope so, because we are straight back into it unless someone has a question.

Themba sighs, "Ready, although I for one am finding this stuff exhausting. What about you oldies? Does it get easier with time?"

Warren replies, "I actually feel a bit lighter. Thanks for listening."

"OK then. There are only two of you left, Themba and Roberto. Who wants to go first?"

Roberto chooses.

I'll go then my timeline is very different from all of you. From early childhood I was uncared for. Even when I could only just walk I had to do for myself. I was put out on the street at fourteen when my dad got a new woman. I had a very hard life. And you know, once you put your feet under another person's table you have to live by their rules.

You know we used to have the milk delivered and we would steal the milk or the milk money. I was naughty.

As a child I began to throw stones at the police and we would burn our furniture. There were riots in Mitchell's Plane. I was at school but we were locked out and our parents were scared. We stood outside the school and the police came in their Casspirs and beat us and set off tear gas. We ran into our houses and they followed us. So we took our furniture to block their way. It was very frightening. I was beaten like a dog and kicked and hit.

After that, the teachers went back to work but they weren't allowed to hit. They lost control and we didn't learn. I left school in standard seven and began selling fruit and vegetables and then I drove a cab. At fourteen I became a painter. I was good and I also learned some plumbing and other skills but they couldn't get me papers because I was too young.

At that time I got disillusioned and began to smoke ganja. I don't smoke it any more but it helps many people with their pain. There was an old man who had cancer and I got some for him. That was the first time he slept through the night. I got it for him until he died.

I blamed my father and the strange things that went on in our home. A neighbour's dogs killed two of my brothers, two others out of the nine ended up in prison. They learned from my father's control to be gangsters. I was scared that their behaviour could lead to murder so I chose another path. I remember I was in a fight at about eighteen. I was under a bridge and I picked up a brick and then put it down. I decided I did not want to cause pain. I would never hurt another.

You know with Mandela people began to make their own choices. There were lots of people on the street but there were schools, fewer gangs. We had a free choice. But then everything got messed up because everyone wants to be a leader and choose when things will start and stop.

I chose the streets. You need to walk this path to understand it. We only have the streets but it is our choice. We also choose not to con people. We are honest but we have nothing. I say be careful what you do under the sun. White people don't believe in God but He will bring you to right. Everyone wants and stealing is part of the world today.

I think about what is right and wrong for myself and choose to walk the straight line and share the little I have with others. I believe that it is right to love one another like oneself. That is heaven on earth. The poor are already in heaven. I believe that with all my heart. We were put here for a reason.

You ask what is most important. Listening is important. Also, don't be scared to face your fears. Non-believers build a bridge because they are scared to swim but swimming makes me a better believer.

I want to see backstage. I believe in God the creator of all creatures. In a tree bearing the fruit of life. God is the Alpha without Omega because he has no end. Eternal life awaits us. When we suffer it is because we bring hell upon ourselves on earth. God brings only good.

I met Ruth when she left her husband and wanted someone to help her go back. That was fifteen years ago. She got a job in the harbour cleaning fish and I was working on the boats. We got a place together, a place of our own. It was only a shack but we kept it clean.

But then the quota system came in and only people who had businesses could get a licence to fish. We got a smaller place, but then we ran out of money and had to sell our furniture to buy food. Then we stayed outside for a while but we still had pride. We always took care of ourselves. Made sure we were clean. People didn't believe us. We showered at the shelter. But then they were closed and we were back to showering in cold water. Our friends lost compassion for us and wouldn't help with food. They always said they had eaten or had nothing. We wouldn't do that. I would rather give someone food out of my own mouth than see them go hungry. That's how I heard about CTT. I was getting food from a café that saves leftovers for us.

There is always something before sunset. We believe in God. He is with us, with or without. We depend only on God. Every minute in every day we pray. We ask God to listen and to take a little pain away. Whoever God blesses no one can curse. He is the only one to set you free. Only through darkness can you find light.

I have learned from Reggae and Gospel music. I am a Rastafah. For fifteen years I have grown my hair and worked at being a good person. I left ganja so that I can live life in the light every day. I appreciate anything whether I earn money or not.

I believe that if someone asks us for our blanket we will give it to him and keep ourselves warm under a thin blanket by huddling together. If people steal from us, we have nothing again. People scratch through our things all the time, but what doesn't kill us makes us stronger. There is no one else to care for us. When we get depressed we cry together. We listen to each other. All we want is unconditional love. We need to love the living things around us like the wind that blows, the sun shining, the stars that come out at night and the rain. I say when Moses comes Moses bring rain to cleanse you. When he puts a foot over the mountain it drizzles, when he puts both feet over it rains hard and when the thunder comes Moses speaks. When day turns to night everyone runs.

The worst thing that happened was when we were sitting at Outspan and saw a small flame burning under the overpass. When we got closer we saw our things burning. Someone had taken gasoline and set all our belongings alight. It was part of us and it was all gone. I went over and came back crying. There was only ash, everything was burned out, all our few belongings. Now all we have left we carry in a bag. We only have one set of clean clothes. I became depressed that night. Then he looked up at us and smiled.

You know only a strong man can cry.

"Thanks so much Roberto. we will move straight on to you, Themba, because we want to get to that walk. We all need it."

I was pleased to keep my story brief starting with my father's death and ending with me coming to CTT. I was amazed at how many similarities there were between my life and that of others.

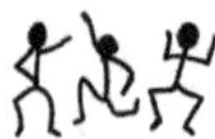

I've had enough and need to escape so I gulp down a glass of milk grab a scone and head for the beach only to find that Warren, Roberto and Soda have beaten me to it.

"Hi I don't know about you guys, but I need a good fast walk to clear my head."

"We'll join you."

I stride off fast and don't look back, but no need, they keep pace. Again the air is fresh, the breeze warm and the spray on the wave crests shimmers in the sun. A few cotton wool clouds deepen the blue sky that meets the corrugated sea in a distant haze. I lose my breath, my anger and my anguish to my full-bodied advance. Metre upon metre of footprints string out behind us, we keep pace, each consumed by his own exertion. As we reach the far end of the beach Warren touches my arm and I stop. He turns away from the sea and points.

"Do you see the dunes? Behind them there is heath then a marshy hollow, behind that a road, a rise, a high fence and then Ocean View. Just out of our sight, an Apartheid joke and we bought it. Now a slum filled with disheartened people, drugs, hopelessness and crime. Those are my people."

I scowl, stand a while and look and then turn back to the sea. "This is my first time at the beach, my second walk, but I will return and bring my family with me. Soda smiles. You would never get any of my guys to come to this side of the city man. It's Greenpoint for us. He dances back down the beach. Roberto smiles as he follows. "He's a good guy, man. Bet he never done a days work in his life. Man after my own heart." I smile and notch up a gear. "We going to be late for dinner if we don't move and I need a shower."

Nalendi

My job as a CTT presenter is twofold. Firstly I take current issues, be they cultural, community or political, to the people and make them clear and relevant. I want to keep my listening public informed and involved in the world around them. Secondly I want them to feel that their views are important. So through talkback we bring people's experiences and opinions to the attention of others. This interchange has exposed me to the sad stories of South Africa for years.

So while Themba is wildly excited about this experiment, I am energised as always at the prospect of being a catalyst. But my engagement is more laid back. I expect to listen to and weave together the themes running through the stories I hear, and to find some link between these experiences, the dramatic revelations of the TRC and our recent history. But I am afraid I am cynical. I believe it is easy to rake over past hurts; it is much more difficult to forgive our oppressors and move forward. Anyway here goes the first time I sit in on a group.

I walk into the group with Peter, and he introduces me to each person in turn. "Nalendi would you mind introducing yourself to everyone again?"

"Sure. I'm Nalendi. I think I have said hallo to each of you last night. I'm sitting in for a while with each group, so that I can get a feel for the work that you guys are doing. I will move from group to group, so please don't feel upset if I walk out on you. It's not that I am disinterested it's just that I need to sit in on each group so I get a feel for what is going on for all participants. Now I will shut up and let you guys get on with your work."

As each member takes their butcher's paper and begin to work on their timeline, I think about my own and find myself being drawn into a contemplative space I seldom enter. By the time Peter asks for a volunteer to begin I actually have to hold myself back. I really want to be part of this process.

After some toing and froing Ayesha begins.

Fifteen years ago I had an earth shattering experience. I was sent by work to see a psychologist who asked 'when do you want to take charge of your life.' I was very depressed because of my husband's behaviour and blamed myself. One night I said to my kids 'don't talk to me about your father, he is responsible for himself.' But for now let me go back to the beginning.

My name is Ayesha. I believe in people and take account of them. I have always done what I can for others.

My family were staunch Roman Catholics. I was obliged to go to church, say the rosary, follow prayer readings, the whole works, but I found no joy in this. My son says he doesn't like the smell of Catholicism. I now send my children to Catholic school to expose them to both religions, Islam and Catholicism. They can decide for themselves later.

I chose to be a Muslim. As a youngster I was free, single and loved partying and drinking. I had a job but no money because I went to work, clocked out and then went straight out to party. As a result I never earned any commissions, could not pay my rent and things were bad.

One day my boss called me in. He had a bank of recording machines set up along his desk. 'Do you know what these are for. They prove that you don't do any work.' My review was bad. I had no money and couldn't pay my rent. I was about to be evicted because of non-payment when my landlord, a Jew, came to look at my place. He was very surprised to find it clean and neat and offered me an amnesty where, if I paid my rent on time, he would allow me to pay him off a small amount each month until I had covered me debt. He was kind and I tried to make things work but I felt so guilty about my debts that I decided to move back home with Gran.

I was returning home from work and driving down Belgravia Road in Athlone when I saw many people along the road preparing for the Haj. While I was in a taxi filled with people I was completely overwhelmed and began to cry. I got to the home of a friend and her boyfriend and told him I wanted to become a Muslim. He said that a neighbour was a Muslim.' "I will take you to see him." We went next door together and asked for help.

The neighbour asked if I knew the Shada and when I said yes he called his wife who took me into the bathroom and taught me how to cleanse myself. She also gave me a robe and a scarf and invited the imam in. He came and with the neighbour's wife, now my protector, with us he asked me why I chose Islam. I sad I was sure that I wanted this so he told me how to dress, pray and a whole list of rules for the good Muslim life. Once I had listened and agreed to abide by all these the imam said that because I had changed religion my name should change. 'We like your name to be as similar as possible and your birth-name. It was Ida. From now on you will be known as Ayesha.'

God touched me that night. It was a beautiful experience. I took on the Shafi'i way and turned my life around completely.

Four months after becoming a Muslim I married Saaid. I stopped drinking and smoking, and my financial life began to flourish. I fell pregnant after another four months. When I went into labour my waters broke immediately and I was in hospital for twenty-eight hours before having a C-section. I had a son.

I didn't see my husband much during my time in hospital and when he did come he came smelling of smoke. He made many excuses for not being around and coming in late. On the fourth day he came in during the day smelling of marijuana. I was shocked and asked why had he gone back to it. He responded 'to celebrate the birth of my son.'

Saaid already had two sons by a previous marriage.

When I got home from the hospital with my brand new baby, Saaid's mum came to stay for a week with his two sons from his previous marriage. They were six and nine. His sister also came with her child. Saaid and I lived in a one-room apartment so you can imagine how crowded it was. And then Saaid's Mum left his two older sons and his sister and child and went off to stay with a friend from Friday until Tuesday. Saaid disappeared from the Thursday until Monday I kept phoning him but the calls would go straight through to voicemail.

He was now back on drugs but I was a newly converted person and just believed him blindly. By the time his Mum left me with his kids Saaid was on crack cocaine. He blamed a friend for buying it for him. Cocaine has no smell so the only way I could tell was that Saaid had severe temper tantrums. Because my family had always fought I thought this was normal. It was part of what I knew.

By the time my son was one month old, Saaid did not come home on weekends. In the second week my cousin fetched me from Athlone by taxi took me to Saaid's work. I walked in, put my breast fed baby into Saaid's hands, and walked out. I drove around for three hours because I couldn't go to my parent's home and had nowhere else to turn. When I got home Saaid was trying to feed the baby with sugar water. I took my son and fed him. Saaid begged my forgiveness. 'There is just so much temptation one person can take before they give in.' I

accepted and offered to help him with his problem. 'No I will be OK!' The next morning Saaid did not come home. By the weekend I was at my wits end. I went to his workplace again. He saw me, ran out, caught a taxi and slipped out of sight. I went home in turmoil.

I got on my knees and prayed my Maghrid prayer. 'I didn't sign up for this Allah. I can't deal with it. Give me a sign. I feel lost and abandoned, all my friends drink. I now wear a scarf. Help me.' I got up, there was a knock at the door and there was the imam who had married me. He had not been to see Saaid or me since we had moved. He said 'Salaam Alaikum, is your husband here?'

I said no, but invited him in. He refused saying he could not if another man was not with them, but I insisted saying that I needed to speak. The imam entered and sat behind a screen.

He listened and said 'when he comes home give him my number and say he must call.'

On Monday evening Saaid returned as if nothing were wrong. He called the imam who took him away to the mosque and then brought him back home. Saaid told me that he was going off on a three-day retreat with the imam the following weekend. He left and came back a believer. He had met with some Maliki believers who were stricter Muslims. Saaid became involved and his behaviour improved. The family flourished; a daughter was born. We started up an NGO teaching kids to surf, moved to Zeekooivlei, then to Fish Hoek in 2010.

I had been working full time but was retrenched in 2008. Until then I had supported Saaid in the NGO by providing meals for the kids. After being retrenched I became more involved with those kids who were not in school and started a class at Fish Hoek library. The kids who had cards would take books home to read and write an essay. The others would read at the library. I was very hands-on and I loved it.

Saaid had never been the family provider. While he worked, his brother moved into the family home. With the ease of getting credit, moving into a bigger house and supporting the surf club, Saaid suggested that I shouldn't worry about owing money to the 'Kafir'. It meant nothing. I didn't realise what I was doing and became arrogant allowing Saaid to go on a spending spree for the NGO creating work for others. I got myself into debt to the tune of R200,000.

By the end of 2009 there was a shift in our relationship. Something was wrong and I was tired. I told Saaid that he needed to get work. It was his turn.

The family would always go to my parents to celebrate Christmas. Christmas Day was also Saaid's birthday, but this time he refused to go. He would do something on his own. I was shocked but we had been fighting so I accepted his decision.

In 2010 life took a bigger bang. In May we took kids on a sponsored trip to Port Elizabeth through the NGO. A young girl came up to Saaid and me, and he introduced her to me as Sally. Sally offered to take care of Paul and thirty minutes later Saaid had disappeared.

After that things went bad. In June I had to be in court for a traffic violation. Saaid took me to court and left me there. 'I will just be going to the imam down the road.' I sat in court thinking what is this? I need him here to support me.

Life continued with Saaid leaving early and coming home late. In July a friend of the family was getting married and Saaid pushed me to invite Sally along. He said she really wanted to see a Muslim wedding. I said I couldn't, the ceremony was an intimate affair, but he insisted so I asked my friend, but then Sally did not go.

In July, Saaid and I were taking kids away to Elandsvlei for the NGO. Sally offered to bring her own car and Saaid wanted to give her money to cover petrol. I refused. This lead to an argument and I didn't go. On their return I saw Sally on the road with my kids in the car. I waved. They had a good time on that trip.

Late in July Saaid asked me for money. He said he could get a good deal for toilet paper which he would on-sell. I argued because this was the only money I had for groceries and the household, but he insists. He dresses well saying he wanted to make a good impression and clinch the deal. That night he came home very late and we don't speak. That weekend he leaves early and tells our son he can't go. He comes home on Sunday night very stressed.

In August there is another camp, this time at Buffalo Bay. Saaid says that my kids can't go because everyone is bunking in together. Saaid's older son had been watching the continual family arguments and was in a bad way. His mum had phoned, worried about him because he was losing out to my kids.

Saaid and his older son sat down together and his son said he wanted to go home to his mother. He said sorry to me but Saaid refused to listen and told his son to get out. There was no support. In the next breath he told me he had found someone else. I was stunned.

Towards the end of July I had this dream. We were in my grandfather's house. He was walking down the passage. I was facing two white women in the kitchen. They were friendly with each other. My grandfather looked very angry, shut the bottom half of a door and I woke, frightened. I kept having worrying dreams and turned to my husband for support but he shrugged me off saying 'why worry about this shit.'

Again he said to me that he had met another woman and I asked where they had met.
Ayesha becomes tearful.

I went and sat in my car struggling to get a grip on what was going on. When my kids came home I put them in Saaid's car saying they could go with him and I drove off.

I lost track of myself. I lived for my family and had more or less cut myself off from my parents because of my change of religion. I had no friends. The only person I could turn to was my sister. I went to her place and saw her boyfriend. He asked me what was going on and I said I'd argued with Saaid. Then I went off to bed. I didn't sleep so I texted Saaid. At seven thirty Sally texted me back to say my kids were OK.

The next day I went through things at work and found receipts for meals. I phoned, but he did not answer so I phoned Sally and asked her if Saaid was with another woman. I called him again. No answer. So I called a male friend who said 'Ayesha, I don't want to be involved but Saaid married another woman two weeks ago.' I gasped put down the phone and rang the Amir and asked 'how can I not know he has married another woman.'

I spoke to Saaid and he said he hadn't married. Then 'I have married her and there is nothing you can do about it.' I was alone at home and breaking all his things and I phoned the imam again and he said he would send his wife to explain about second marriages. I told her I was betrayed but she said I must accept it. 'But I didn't know.' Then I thought back, 'Oh my God, when I was in court he told me he had to see that imam.'

As time went on many people told me to calm down. Then I drove to Wynberg and people explained where that imam lived. I told him 'I'm here to talk about Saaid's wedding.' He smiles 'It isn't every woman who accepts a second wife.'

'Accept! I didn't know. He did not have my permission.'

The imam said, 'but Saaid told me that I could not refuse to marry him. I asked if his first wife knew and he gave me the R300 gratuity for the wedding. I didn't know he was married. Many people were here from around the world to support him.' Shocked, he told me to go to my own mosque. He then went through his book and said 'you must accept it.'

Crying I replied, 'But he didn't adhere to the rules. He married an eighteen-year old white girl. This woman is a child. I trusted her with my children.'

Later I threatened Sally, 'Where do your family live?' Saaid told me 'In Constantia.' Her family are good people. I said, 'I want you to come home.' He didn't come and I got more and more frantic. People told me to calm down but I couldn't. I phoned Sally's mother 'Do you know that my husband married your daughter.' She begged me not to tell her husband. 'He will kill Saaid.' I complied, only to find out later that she and Sally were talking to each other all through this time. Now Sally's parents are divorced because of Sally's marriage and her sister won't talk to her. It is a sad affair.

Can you believe it? My husband did exactly what he did to me to his first wife. He married a younger woman. I decided I would not see him any longer, but I encourage my children to talk to their father. It is important for them to have a relationship with him and to respect his new wife.

The bastard! How could you let him get away with this?

That's why I'm telling you this story so you understand what happens to Muslim women in their marriages. Later he took an intervention order out against me. In court I asked the judge 'if I was so violent why did he leave the kids with me?'

"Did the judge support you?" Ayesha laughed.

No, and the funniest thing was that while all this was happening there was an article in the paper about me and Saaid and 'our wonderful welcoming home where all who came were loved and cared for.' I was a horrible person. These were the worst two to three years of my life.

Six months later I got a call from Saaid 'I am sorry. I want my family back. Please can we meet.' I agreed to meet but just before our meeting there was a text saying Saaid would be late. Later I found out that he used these texts to show others that I was harassing him. When I heard this, my life simply fell apart.

I phoned home and said that I wasn't coming home because I was going off to kill myself. I bought a huge amount of aspirin and some bottled water. A guy followed me to Constantia to a grave where Muslims go to pray. He tried to talk to me but I insisted that if he didn't leave I would crash my car into his. He left saying he would pray for me. I took many pills and in an intoxicated state I began to speak to God. 'I am not weak I don't want to kill myself. Save me.' I woke up the next morning to blue skies but unfortunately I failed the driving test.

I went back home and people formed a shield around me. My work contract ended at the end of March. I still had an enormous debt. I had to cook and clean for others and sell clothes to live. I reached out to Allah in desperation. I was severely depressed and overwhelmed by sadness. I couldn't block out my memories and just wanted to walk into the sea and be done.

In 2012 I met John who was starting a restaurant. He offered me extra work so that I could begin to pay off my debts. I was still angry, but with John's help I was growing. Then one day as I sat in the mosque I suddenly realised that nothing happens by accident. I was not in charge. God was the only planner. My blinkers fell off and I realised that our separation was in God's will. I was trying to make Saaid what he was not. My only reason for living is to rely on God not Saaid. It was not up to me to make him what I wanted. I asked God to help me with my pain and understood that in the moments of my deepest sadness or biggest joy I must remember God.

Things were difficult but I forced myself to rely on God who is always there to help. Now I forced myself to rely on Him, be with Him, think of Him. Now this comes automatically and I have become so much stronger. As I became more content and got things in balance my kids were able to relax. I still struggle, but know that hope lies in remembering God continuously. We have to pray five times a day and sin as little as possible in between. This is how I live my life now. I live by the moment and if I stray I ask forgiveness. I now understand me. The help I got from a homeopath, psychologist, psychiatrist and raki master was wonderful. Now I know others can help and encourage friends to get help with unlocking themselves when they are lost. I understand now that the mind affects the body and the body the mind. You know I bled for ten months, but as I opened myself up to learning I healed and the bleeding stopped. I understand now that we can learn from and teach each other. I teach my kids this. The Muslim religion doesn't allow one to look down on another. God is the judge and we should do unto others, as we would have them treat us. I find now that as I put myself in God's hands and see myself as important to him and look after myself, he gives me strength. He will not give me more than I can handle.

She looked at each of us.

God is at the centre. The ocean ebbs and flows. God is there and our lives are predestined.

Wow! I'd heard many stories about the impact of second and third marriages on the wives and children of Muslim marriages so this story wasn't new but somehow sitting with

Ayesha as she invited us into the centre of her pain made it different; her utter powerlessness, Saaid's emotional and financial violence, the imam's support of this unbelievable behaviour. I bit back my tears. There'd been quite a bit recently about Muslim marriage and Sharia law and this would certainly be worth following, including Ayesha's heartfelt story. But now I sat frozen, surprised by my beating heart, the flowing tears and my reluctance to leave. There was so much I wanted to ask and to say. When Peter moved us on I wasn't ready but I sat back. This wasn't my domain. I wasn't in control here.

"Can I go next because my story sort of follows" Ruth asked?

"Sure."

I finished my matric, fell pregnant and married by twenty. He was a very abusive man who continually accused me of having affairs. I was in and out of hospital all the time. I had depression because of the violence. You know many people don't understand depression but it is a very real illness. It was made worse by the violence.

"Why did you stay?"

I asked myself why, and I did it for my children. I wanted them to have a father. I know it wasn't my fault but there was no love.

I had two kids, a boy and a girl. First I had Natalie and then I fell pregnant with twins. Because of the violence they were born at five and a half months. I gave birth on 10 May and one died on the 11th and the other on 12th. They would have been twenty-one now and I get sentimental still, especially at this time.

Then I fell pregnant again immediately and Bobby was born. They didn't believe me and I had to go from hospital to hospital to get the death certificates for the twins as proof that Bobby could be mine. Bobby was in hospital for two and a half months because his lungs weren't fully developed and he was asthmatic. I had to take him to hospital often and once when I did this I had to lie and say to the staff there that I had walked into a door because I had a black eye . . . it was very bad.

When Bobby was four I fell pregnant again. I was then hospitalised for depression but when I was six months pregnant I ran away. James was born three and a half months premature. His lungs were not fully developed and he could not swallow milk properly. He died at three and a half months and they said it was a cot death. They said he died of 'natural causes.' I rushed him to hospital but when we got there his heart was still beating but they said he was 'brain dead'. While this was all happening my husband had an affair and I was very hurt. I went back into hospital. We were only together for a year after that when I finally said that this time I was leaving for good. I left Natalie with my mum because she was safe there and Bobby with his dad. I wanted them to have a stable life and I wasn't sure where I would be living.

It took me three years to divorce my husband because I had no money and went through the government system. I had eleven different lawyers. I took nothing with me, just the clothes I was standing up in and was in and out of hospital at the time.

I only got better when I met Roberto. He listened to me and put up with all my yelling and screaming. He was my medicine. I could not have children with him because of all the things that had happened to my body in the past.

You know depression is a real illness. There were many times that I felt very low. I had seven nervous breakdowns. You see these marks on my arms. These are where I cut myself with a knife so that I wouldn't hurt so much inside.

My worst time was when my sister died. I was so sad. You know I weighed one hundred kilos but I lost forty through grief. I can't talk about it.

Ruth turned aside with tears streaming down her cheeks.

It's also very hard when I look for work and people promise they will get back to me and then they don't. That really hurts.

I am a good person. I am clean and I can work hard and I know many things but I can't get work and it hurts.

And your best time?

My best is that how ever cold and sad I am I wake the next day healthy. I love it when I have a bit to spare and I can cook for others. I have a good clean heart. I love that I have compassion.

The room is silent. How can I walk out now?

Peter finally breaks the spell by turning to Ruth . "Thank you. It's hard to believe that you have been through all that and are still standing."

Only just I feel like running out of here and going to Khayelitsha to get some real hard drugs right now.

Ayesha goes over to Ruth and hugs her and Ruth bursts into tears. "Nobody hugs me. You all think I'm too dirty. Careful you might catch something." Ayesha smiles and keeps on hugging. The rest of us hang back awkwardly until Peter suggests that a cup of tea may be good. Ruth still clings to Ayesha while the rest of us leave. I wonder how the next participant will follow those two stories. Well, I guess I'll never really know. What I have learned very quickly is that it is one thing to manage people and their stories on air but another to actually put aside all else and truly hear how people live with tragedy. I for one am so focused on the community that sometimes people's personal misery escapes me.

Having left Ruth and Ayesha with my heart in my mouth, I don't go in to morning tea. I go to my room to think. If I'm to manage this weekend as part of a project I'll need to get back in touch with the observer role. I can't be overwhelmed by everything I hear.

So four groups to go, and about an hour for each story. That's three hours in four groups if Themba can tell me about the vibe in his, so an hour in each of the remaining groups.

The devil I know

It's so much easier as an observer. I go in and ask the group to ignore me. Ali is already talking and no one even acknowledges my entry.

Well, what we face is ostracism. Our opportunities have always been restricted. My parents were poor but they worked hard to educate me. I went to PenTech and did a diploma in marine architecture. You know 'Coloured Education' was always second-class. It was designed to keep us oppressed. Many subjects were simply not beneficial.

"It must have been hard to keep going when you knew classes were a waste of time."

"Oh come off it Sue. Of course there were three tiers of education. I fought like hell to go to Grahamstown because I just wasn't prepared to get a second-class university degree. You must know that you whites always did and still have access to the best. Both you and the blacks stole everything from us Khoi-San and that gave you what you have today."

"I don't want to stop Ali's story but I do want you to know, Marti, that I came from a very poor Afrikaans family and I had to work my way through university."

Simon put his hand up between them. "Come on girls give Ali a go!"

Well, actually it started long before PenTech. I grew up in District Six in a settled, multicultural community, at the foot of Table Mountain, close to work and the city but when I was eight or nine we were forcibly removed. We were told our land would be used to build a highway. Our removal to Athlone was very traumatic and living became much harder. Everything was more expensive there and Dad travelled long distances to his work as an artisan. We hardly saw him.

My parents were strong people and with five kids we pulled together as a family. We were Muslims and my older brother supported my dad as the oldest son until he died in an accident at about twenty-seven. Then it became my job to help the family. When Dad retired his pension was only R37 a month and it became my job to help carry the obligations of the family. When Dad died Mum lived on in the house he had built for them, but when she got dementia she came to stay with us. She was with us for eleven years before she died.

Apartheid was hard on us with whites only benches, shops and toilets. Life was very restricted, impossible really, so we didn't go anywhere, but in a way it did us a favour because in defending against Apartheid we learned to stick together and support each other. We began to work at keeping our money within our communities. We built shops, businesses and factories and became self-sufficient. We also entertained ourselves. We had tremendous music and the whole community would get involved in the 'coloured' rugby unions with matches played in Athlone and at Greenpoint almost becoming festivals. We knew how to enjoy ourselves.

These fizzled out at the end of Apartheid.

We became very protective of our own and when people came in from outside and misused our trust we would let them know that they weren't welcome.

My son had two white teachers. One guy used to come roaring in on his bike. When we found out that he got a white salary and a 'danger allowance' the kids let him have it. Violence breads violence you know.

"Nothing has changed. There is violence all the time on the flats, violence and gangs and Tik. Our community is eating itself alive."

"I tried to help a fellow shake Tik." Simon responds. But after taking him away from it and offering him a home and work he ran back to it. A waste of my money and time. It's a bloody scourge, Tik and it's sending many young people psychotic and violent." Simon then turns to Ali, "sorry for interrupting mate."

Ali nods.

Where was I? Oh yes. When Mandela first came in, he stabilised everything. We have a beautiful constitution and Mandela was well supported by Trevor Manuel his finance minister. If only we complied with our constitution. And to me Manuel was a natural choice for Mandela's replacement when he stood down but that didn't happen because the ANC wanted a black man. Things slipped after that. Now they are as tough as ever they were under Apartheid.

"Worse I reckon!"

But I have no regrets. I gave my children as good an education as I could afford and they are all doing well. I would have loved better opportunities and I find it difficult when people with less education get promoted above me. You see Apartheid is still alive and well. But I have respect within my community. I am a trustee of seven mosques. As a Muslim I believe my destiny is in the hands of Allah. We are given our life and must make the most of it.

In a way Apartheid has created many opportunities. For example Mitchell's plane is a sandy wasteland but the people have said 'we are here now what must we do.' The first thing they did was to establish places to pray. There are now 39 mosques. Alhamdulillah, praise be to God. Now there are businesses, manufacturing, steel works and they did it all themselves.

"And gangs and corruption and shootings and killings."

"Give it a break Sue, you will have your turn."

Ya, corruption is rife, there are massive drugs problems and as you know crystal meth is pernicious. And now the vigilante groups have been banned things are not safe at all.

But thank God none of my kids were involved in drugs and I put this down to their mother being at home always. She is a housewife and has always been there for them. In other families both parents worked and the children have not had the support they needed.

For example, under Apartheid, when my son was about seven he was playing cricket behind the school when two Casspirs just drove up and parked in the field opposite the school.

Next thing they were shooting rubber bullets and spraying the kids with tear gas and they all had to run. My son ran back into the school toilets. He kept knocking but they wouldn't let him in to any stalls because they thought he was the police after them. He said he couldn't breathe. Tear gas smells ten times stronger than ammonia. His eyes were burning. Mucus was streaming from his nose. He was very frightened.

But then his Mum was there to take him home from school. When I came home my son told me and I comforted him and told him he had managed a dangerous situation well. The next day he went back to school. We got through things together and survived.

My children were well cared for, their mother was a housewife she put the family first. She was always there.

God is always there!

We are not on earth just to enjoy the fruits. We must also give something back. And all those things, like the smash and grabs, they are part of life. Life is given to us by Allah, to be lived and we must get on with it.

"So we must just accept life?"

That's not what I said! Ali mutters through drawn lips.

A dominance dance is brewing; the air is electric and I want no part of it. I slip out quietly, and unobserved I hope.

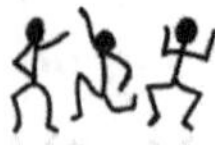

About half an hour to lunch, I stop, stretch and swallow sea soaked air. I might grab a solitary coffee on the terrace. The stories, uninhibited and outside my control, sap my strength. Do these facilitators know their business?

I walk through the door and there she sits hunched on the second step. She is focused on tracing a nail hole with her index finger oblivious of sea, sand or sky. I want to shake her and yell, "look up and out, taste the salt in the air, feel the breeze."

"What's wrong Ruth?"

No movement no raised face, no recognition. I sit. "Ruth?" Tears stain her cheeks, she quakes "Go away!" Thank God she's still here. "OK, I'll go as soon as I know what's up."

"The memories swallow me. I sink, drown with each death and now there's nowhere to turn, every face reflects back my misery. I can't fucking forget, can't escape. You'll all pursue me, slime me with kindness then walk away and leave me fighting for air, alone."

I sit sandwiched between this heaven and her hell. I feel the slime, want to rush off and shower away the sticky shame. What am I doing here away from the safe encapsulating walls of the studio? What to do, what to say, how to escape? "So there is nothing I can do?"

"No nothing!"

I sit. How long? I stretch out a hand to touch Ruth but she flinches. Moves away as if I will strike. I need to escape. There's no reaching her and the slime will pull me down, cover my head, and suffocate me. And then she shivers, quakes free, rasps, "It's me. I killed them, my badness destroys everything I touch." and her tears wash down her dark cheeks and drip off her chin. What is there to say? I want to agree with her, confirm her fear, say yes your yuck is all consuming. It kills!

She looks up now at the sky "this is why I came. You said on radio that if we share our stories and seek forgiveness together things could get better for our country. Well, I hope you're right 'cause you don't want to drown with me."

"No, well that's what we're hoping."

Consumed I have not heard the others coming. Ayesha sits on the step below and smiles. "Hey Ruth, come on sweetie." She looks up and smiles and I take my leave and head for my room. Here I yank off my shoes get into bed and pull my covers over my head. What the hell have I got myself into?

Instruction

Themba sits in the one free spot at the dinner table and looks around. Nalendi catches his eye and smiles. Her face is drawn and her big brown eyes look tired, or has she been crying? Bobotie, great! He is ravenous. He looks around the table "water anyone" and settles back.

Warren is speaking "I have noticed themes of issues. Displacement is a big one. Not surprising as it was the corner stone of Apartheid policy but I'm also hearing about corruption, quotas and mismanagement of government today, robbery and gang violence, drug and alcohol abuse (especially Tik) and family violence . . ."

"What'd we do without our teacher hey?" chimes in Soda.

"But it's true, man and don't forget street crime and murder on the flats."

"Ja, I was visiting my cousin three weeks ago in Manenberg and there was this street gang and they were shooting man. One bullet whizzed past very close to my car. We drove in to . . ."

I switched off. We hear these stories all the time. I was much more interested in the themes Warren was talking about and the Bobotie. The yellow rice with nuts and raisins smells 'lecker,' the Bobotie is moist and the chutney to die for.

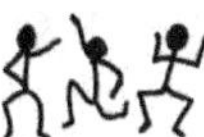

Just as I relaxed back after melktert and coffee we are ushered into the big training room. I turn to Soda. "I'm too tired for this."

"OK please get into your groups, turn to your partner and talk about how you are feeling now and how you felt when you shared in your group."

I looked around and sigh, "OK Soda you and me?"

Soda twinkles, "You too damn depressing man, so we'll start with me." I look deep into his wrinkled face, each South African season has etched another deep furrow into his brow and the skin around his mouth is sculptured into an eternal cheeky smile but the honey brown eyes are deep and sad and his mouth twitches.

"OK shoot."

"It feels good to be here man. I am excited. There's a buzz. People think this is important and I get to hang out with you. Normally you black guys just tell me to get lost. There is no space for an old Griqua in this new black world man. Never before have I heard people talking about their lives like I have today, makes you seem almost human." He thumps my shoulder and winks. "I wonder what's next. Maybe they're just softening us up for the kill. What do you think, man? Get us all lovey-dovey and then put the boot in? . . . Oh I forgot, you one of them aren't you. Maybe I said too much."

I can't help laughing, "Come on Soda, lets get into this. I want it to work."

"Well, I've been hurting with you other guys man. My life has been tough but it's hard to open up and give you a chance to punch man. I learned long ago to keep my fists up. When I don't, I'm scared man! Scared that I'm getting old and I can't face another winter in my windy old Bo-Kaap and no one wants me to hang around the house and my old mates are dying and my teeth hurt and I'm crying on the inside because my family want to sell our place and . . . oh hell it's bloody hard man and I feel like shit. But my smile keeps you out and while I'm dancing you can't get to clout me. That's it man!" He looks down and his sagging jaw shakes. "Your turn to stick out your chin, come on Themba."

"Wow! I'm sorry Soda. I'd never have guessed all that stuff. You OK for me to go? I'm pretty raw myself. I always thought no one understood what it was like to lose yourself to grief but what I've seen today is that we all lost so much because of Apartheid. I lost my father, but others lost their home and their compass and their courage. I'm so sad and I want to run. I want to hide. I don't want to hear what happened to other people I want someone to put their arms around me and say "sorry Themba, sorry you lost your father and your mother and who you are. Sorry people make fun of you, sorry that they interfered with your manhood and made you associate your penis with pain. Sorry you don't earn enough to bring your wife and kids to Cape Town." I hold my stomach as I begin to shake and the tears run. Soda extends his hand and I clasp it tightly, gulp for breath and begin to still myself. "That's how I feel. I didn't know it but that's how I am. And scared Soda, so scared about what will happen in the group. I don't like this. It's too risky for me too."

We sit a moment and realise that the group is waiting for us. "Are you ready to talk to the whole group?" I sit stunned but Soda jumps to the rescue, "Sure man I'll show you mine if you show me yours." Others laugh and then in turn each responds. Linda has found the group enlightening and enjoyed broadening her experiences by fitting other stories alongside her own. She smiles "I have been deeply touched by each, your openness and generosity." Warren extends his gaze to include each of us. "I have been taken by the commonality of our stories. It is heartwarming to recognise our important histories and to acknowledge what each of us has lost to Apartheid." Roberto smiles, "I am sad about the stories but I know that only a strong man can cry. I think this work is important to God and whoever weeps will not do so in vain."

We are then asked to think about the common themes running though our stories. Trust Warren. I already know him well enough to expect his anticipation of the weekend's direction. "Each of us has either been displaced or set apart by Apartheid policies, whether by eviction or at a broader level by being thrown off a bus, not allowed to sit on a public bench or prevented from peeing in a public toilet. Displacement must be our number one theme!"

Still caught in sadness and isolation I name them as themes. Everyone nods and on queue Soda says, "You got me man, and I got your back!" He jumps to his feet does a pirouette and sits. We smile acknowledging the comic relief he works at for each of us. "Resilience" Linda says and this is added to our list. "Cruelty" Warren adds and we are done. We sit together and wait.

Simon stands. "We have shared from our hearts today and listening has allowed us to open our hearts. Remember that we have all committed ourselves to confidentiality. This means that no one tells another's story or speaks of it behind another's back."

Simon walks towards the board and writes as he speaks. "Terrible things happen but each of us has a choice to hold on to the pain and become bitter and want revenge or to heal and forgive."

Don, whom I haven't had a chance to speak to yet, asks, "So how do we heal?"

"Healing begins with being heard."

"We've been doing that all day!"

"Yes and we all know the old questions 'Where was God, why do the innocent suffer and the guilty get off easily?'

"Tomorrow morning we will have a ceremony together to help us appreciate the journeys we've been on and to think about what steps each of us may need take towards healing."

"We will silently name our losses, then light a taper to symbolise our grief and stand together for a minutes silence to honour our losses. We will then write on a slip of paper what we would like to leave behind, spend a few moments thinking on these and then, without sharing, throw the scrap into a fire. Finally each group will contribute something like a song, a poem, a drawing, or a dance. Chat to your group and decide what you will do. That's a lot but for now lets party."

I turn to Soda "I hate ceremonies."

"Well I don't, come on and I'll teach you how to boogie you old man." He jumps to his feet and dashes for the centre of the room. I follow "Every Zulu man knows how to dance. I'll show you."

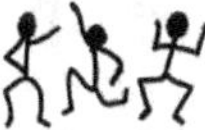

I fall into bed exhausted. The dancing was great and everyone boogied with us but tomorrow promised new challenges. Forgiving is not my strong suit.

I am dancing again but this time alone. The air is dank and I stir dust from the dirt floor as my feet pound to the sound of drum beats. The world closes in. Sheets of pounding rain block my exit from a familiar cave. I bump against the rough sloping roof and shadowy forms writhe, rise from their prone positions, creep out of the rock wall and begin to dance around me. They sing in clicks to the beat of my drums. *"We are the Aboriginals, the First Nation peoples and you have plundered and stolen our land."*

They weave in and out coming closer and then parting as if to allow my escape but at any sign of my moving they bounce closer and their chanting increases.

My chest tightens, my penis stands erect and I prepare to fight or flee, but just as I draw in breath to pounce Soda is there saying, "Come on man relax, go with it man." I cry out "Nooooo . . ." but before I can regroup I am shaken awake. Nalendi stands wrapped in her dressing gown "Hey Themba, wake up. You were screaming. Are you OK?"

I struggle to wake. Nalendi touches my arm and I recoil. "Hey Themba, it's me." She stands back and I struggle to a sitting position. She smiles, "Bad dream huh. I couldn't sleep, how about some tea?"

We make tea and move on to the balcony. The darkness is ink black with stars glittering so close I could pluck them from the sky. The sea foams silver and thunders kettledrum crescendos behind the rustling scrub where crickets chirp. We sit wordless consumed by the night and after a timeless tea each returns to bed. I now sleep till morning.

From past to future

After breakfast, Simon stands "We began by thinking about our journeys in the past, about what has affected us. Yesterday we shared some of our journeys with each other. Today, we'll look toward our future. What are our hopes for ourselves and our communities and what are our next steps towards healing?"

He leads us across the room "What we have here is some clay, and we would like you to sit silently and make a container to hold a candle symbolising your hopes and dreams for yourself, your family, your community."

I sit alone and shape my clay as taught by Umkhulu into a bull with broad back, humped shoulders, big head and sharp horns. In his back I shape a deep hollow to fit the candle. As I do so I remember my life as herd boy, grandson and protector of my sister. I remember my rural life near the Drakensburg Mountains and the promise that life will always be contained, comfortable and circumscribed.

Nothing foreshadowed the turmoil of my teens, or the loss of self that was to come. I am totally absorbed by the task at hand and so sad, dejected, lost. Can I let this go? I smooth the surface of my bull, shape his flaring nostrils, pinch his eyes and focus on his large appendage. My bull has what it takes. He will carry my regret and make way for my future. He has the power . . .

Soda taps me on the shoulder, "Come on man Simon says . . ."

I shake myself into the present.

"I would like you to move into your groups and work on your contribution to be shared in our joint liturgy. Remember to think first about what poison you wish to leave behind and then create and practice your symbol."

As soon as we settle in our group Warren begins to speak. "I have been thinking about the poison I wish to leave behind all night. I have never let our dispossession get me angry because I see no point to anger."

"What I have done is work to rebuild our community wherever I could. That is why I went into teaching and fought for the rights of my people to a first class education. It's why I keep my extended family under one roof and it's why I hope our home is kept as a legacy for my family. We have been scattered, and bringing my family together under one roof keeps our history alive for me . . . But the bottom line is that we are scattered far and wide and it is very difficult now to know my extended family.

"My faith is very important and I believe this is why I work to support my church. A lot of our family are saved. We are very active in the Church in Ocean View and I've been instrumental in building there but there is no follow through. The culprits are actually the people who come into the church and claim they are helping. They don't talk about the Lord, they focus on 'We will get you money for this or that.' instead of the spiritual healing of the people. They mean well, but they don't live in the community and they upset things. They destroy but are under the impression that they help.

"I guess what I am saying is that I would like to find a way to symbolise our need to regain our identity as God's people, as an inclusive nation rather than as a splintered population of the displaced and dispossessed."

I think of my dream. I was completely trapped by being a descendant of those who had slaughtered others. Would their ghosts get me? My shame paralyses me, traps me as a perpetrator. But I lost my father to some meaningless power struggle and am its victim. I feel angry, sad, and powerless . . . and yet I am a contributor. I have helped to bring about this workshop, so in a way I am powerful. I am so mixed up. How do I make sense of all this for myself and for the group? "Warren I think I am stuck like some of your church members. I want to get rid of my poison."

Linda looks at me, and smiles. "I think we all feel trapped by the poison of dispossession. That is why we work so hard at honouring what we lost. That is what the District Six Museum is all about, and it's why I spent so much time there. First we collected the history and all the artefacts we could and of course we began to write the histories. This is about identity. And for me it was as I took others on tours of what was District Six that I began to pick up little treasures I found in the dirt. An old marble, a spinning top, buttons, an old cotton reel, and found a place for these in my memory box; as I sorted and cleaned and conserved I grew more resolved.

"This worked so well for me that I began to lead other people on a similar journey where they collected things that reminded them of their lost past and they began to build small collections and to talk about these and to heal. And then I was invited to America where I went to the Smithsonian and talked about my work and now there are others who collect and conserve as a way of regaining identity. This is a powerful symbolic process and perhaps one we can share with others here."

Soda dances around as he listens. "What can we find? Lets go man and search."

"No hang on Soda, lets continue to track the group. What about you, Roberto?" He smiles, "Ya, it was the same poison for me. I left home at fourteen and since then I have been roaming, a displaced soul known only to God. He is my all in all. I suppose for me with my Ganja it's the forbidden way of buying redemption. But as I told you all, if I didn't sell it to people in pain they would suffer like hell. And now for years people have looked for me at the harbour man and I sell them what they need to still the pain. I know from God this is the right thing to do, so if you need it for your health I will sell it to you. But at the heart of what each man should do is to find his God given identity, so I'm with Soda. A symbol for each person and a short explanation of what it is for."

I'm still struggling my dream from last night, so as my way of joining the group I tell them of the poison I saw in my dream.

"I am trapped because I see myself as a proud Zulu warrior, and it is only right that the ANC is in power and that my people are given a helping hand even if that makes me a 'quota man'. In fact, I lost my father to the cause and my mother to necessity. But at the same time in my dream I see that I come from a nation who have killed others to establish ourselves. So in this I am responsible and complicit. I am trapped by this history and am shamed by my inability to stand up without help. I cannot work out a comfortable identity, so I too need to be saved from the displacement this country has visited on me and would like to find a symbol to lead me forward."

Soda jumps in. "That leaves only me, and I have been running always, here and there to duck the restrictions the Apartheid government placed on me. And now I find no difference, as again I do not fit. I'm a forgotten remnant of a mixed up people and what I see is half Griqua and half a mix of who knows what from where. I don't have a trade or work to do and if I stray too far from my colourful Bo-Kaap I fear I will be lost, nothing. So what will we say to the rest of the crew to go with our symbol of longed for identity? Lets work it out, you guys are good at that and I will go hunt my prey and get my thrills by bringing home a token that will fit the bill."

Linda and Warren look at each other and laugh. Warren says, "Seems like we've got our contribution. How about a simple statement? . . ."

We work on a short speech.

"Sounds great!"

I rise and put my arm around Soda, "Can we go and find our symbol?" The others nod, Soda dances ahead and I follow. He heads directly into the scrub behind the building. "It's the wrong time of year for seed pods." Then he pushes on a while through the tangled scratchy scrub, stops and says, "Look, perfect!" Before him is a small clearing and on the ground, lit by a shaft of sun light are a million white sea pebbles. He throws a handful up at the sky, then we bend and carefully select thirty of the most perfect round pebbles we can see and carry them back to our group. "Look what we found!" We all hug. Our group rocks.

We are first in to morning tea.

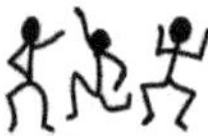

After morning tea, we move onto the balcony for the farewell ceremony. We are each handed a pen and a piece of paper. "You have each now had time to think about the poison you wish to leave behind. On your paper write the word or a short sentence describing the toxin . . . now scrunch it into a ball and when you are ready toss it into the flames.

I write in bold angular letters

MY LIFE WAS STOLEN WHEN DAD WAS KILLED

angrily crunch the paper and throw it into the fire. Then I stand back and breathe heavily as others do likewise. The silence is profound as even the rumble of the sea fades. I choke back the tears.

We stand in silence for a minute when the last person has thrown their paper on the fire then each of us carries our clay creation into our workroom. I am so proud of my perfect bull. It represents so much of my beginnings, of my history of who I am.

Its weight is lighter than I expect but the texture is cool and solid against my skin and slightly scratchy. I have not smoothed the surface as I did as a child when I would wash it with water to give it a glossy finish. This is right. The texture heavy and raw like my anger and pain. How dare South Africa steal my father, my safety, my future. I am completely absorbed by these overwhelming facts. How can I forgive and forget? How can I let go of the fuel that has driven me for so long? I have been wronged. My attitudes are justified. I'm . . . Hot tears burn my cheeks as I stand and stare at the centre of the room, unaware of my fellows. How do I let go of my poison and why should I forgive and forget?

Simon stands in front of me and stops to light my candle from his burning taper. He looks deep into my eyes and waits for me to bring my candle forward to flame. I hesitate but then as a waft of waxy smoke reaches my nostrils I move towards the flickering flame. As my candle lights Simon smiles, then moves on and stops before Linda who stands by my side.

I refocus on the flame in front of me and wait until invited to place my bull alongside the other tokens. Slowly I lower myself and let my bull go as I mutter under my breath. I will try and forgive those who trespassed against me. I will try to forgive myself also. I stand shuddering and hope no one sees my profound loss.

Then slowly I look around. Others also cry. Some are muttering. I am but one of many standing before God trying to separate myself from my painful past. I look up through the window and out at the sea. A breeze whispers through the leaves, sun shines brightly in the clear blue sky, I am back in the present and excited to begin our next activity.

We sit on the floor in a wide circle and Simon speaks. "Forgiveness is difficult, but we separate ourselves from the poison not for others but to set ourselves free. Free to live fulfilled lives. Please remember that what we have done today is to take the first step towards freedom."

We sit silently for several moments and then Simon asks which group would like to begin by bringing their contribution to our joint ceremony.

Of course Soda jumps up and says, "We want to begin. We have something for you." He stands before each person, in turn and hands him or her a shiny white beach pebble. When he is done Warren stands and reads our statement.

South Africans seem to have lost their sense of identity because of the many ravages of the Apartheid regime. We have now become the rainbow nation but we have not yet dealt with our shame or guilt. While some people began to tell their stories to the Truth and Reconciliation Commission, this work was not completed or offered to the average man.

We believe that our country needs to find a way to help her citizens find a comfortable new identity and we offer each person here this symbol of our longed for civil identity.

Each person looked at their pebble, most rub and polish theirs for a while obviously taking in the words and relating strongly before one and then another slips their stone into a pocket.

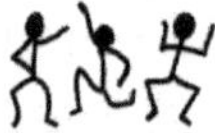

Then Sienna steps forward. "I think our poem follows on from your statement. It raises issues that have overwhelmed the Cape Flats where people were dumped unceremoniously by the Apartheid government when they were taken from their homes. Ali ,would you like to read to us?"

"Sure!"

Gangsters of the Cape Flats by Samuel Damons

We are the gangsters of the Cape Flats.

We used to stay in places like Bo-Kaap, Landsdowne and Kensington

I am a gangster of the Boston kids

And with other's we don't mixed.

In the early years our brothers used to fight with knives, but now it's the gun, and to die is fun.

If there's no dagga and drugs to smoke.

We will brake in houses and kill even murder.

Apartheid is part to be blamed.

And when we die, all they say (Ag) it's a shame.

Some of us used TIK and other cocaine.
That's better than wine they said.

Sometimes brother will stand up against brother
just for one drug,

that could corrupt,

Dying will turn to pain because
smoking drugs become their game.

Here in South Africa, if you play with the gun,
you die by the gun.

Never mind what other's say

We kill and never think.

Kill me quick is the place where we stay.

Here we fight till the bodies lay.

Cape Flats here we come

We are gangsters and that's fun.

We sit quietly and wait.

"This poem captures the pain of people who were not able to survive the shadows of our history. Thank you."

Again we sit and each of us reflects on those souls lost to our history for a few moments before the next group speaks.

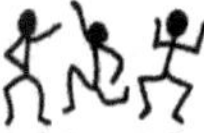

Each person within our group has faced personal traumas, but we all felt that one scourge wrecks generation upon generation and brings devastation to our society. Family violence is an overwhelming issue and the powerlessness of women within our country must be addressed.

We bring the reality of this issue to you by saying that for one person within our group family violence led to a premature birth and the death of a child. Another consequence of ongoing abuse is depression and mental illness. For another group member it brought on isolation a total loss of identity, an attempted suicide and years of sadness and regret.

Firstly, we want to talk about the different kinds of abuse. Ruth wants you to know that she did not only face physical abuse but also verbal taunts, hurts and put-downs. The broken bones and bruises led to many hospitalisations and to the premature birth of a baby. This in turn led to Ruth's flight from the relationship and to homelessness and loss of contact with her children. "I was never well enough myself to be a good mother and this means that my children don't trust me now. And because of this they are broken people. This poison will never leave me. It is good to have youse listen to me but the pain is not going to go."

Other types of violence leave no physical bruises but the results are just as devastating. Ayesha wants the world to know that the consequences are severe and ongoing also. "I want to talk about the institutional violence condoned by some Islamic practices and say that it breaks women emotionally." Ayesha's husband took drugs, lied to her, isolated her, had an affair and married a new younger woman without Ayesha knowing, took the family's financial resources to support his own habits, leaving the rest of the family with no money for food, and implicated and involved religious leaders in his subterfuge. The poison Ayesha continues to fight against is that her entire womanhood was undermined; she lost all sense of self and finally attempted suicide.

So in Ayesha and Ruth's stories we catalogue physical, social, emotional, financial and verbal abuse all as different aspects of the same thing. In both stories there was no space for them as individuals and they were both abused because they were women and had no power or acceptance of themselves in their own right.

Our group brings to the liturgy a clear naming of violence and domestic violence as a poison and against the law. We honour Ayesha and Ruth and support them in their desire to talk openly about this ubiquitous problem. These are two brave woman and we believe the telling of their stories publicly is important.

We also encourage Ayesha in her desire to bring her concerns to the broad attention of Muslim leaders. For too long, too many Muslim women in the Cape and possibly further afield have suffered because these issues are not discussed openly within the Islamic leadership.

We stand with Ayesha and Ruth. Women have the right to be equal and family violence is no private matter. It is simply wrong and against the law.

Everyone is hushed. Simon walks up to Ayesha and Ruth in turn and says "thank you each for your bravery in speaking out."

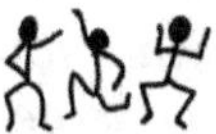

Again silence and then Chris stands to read for his group." Our contribution is in response to the fear that has spilled over in our lives in the last few years. We bring as a token to the liturgy, our dream."

We have walked too long in fear's shadow. Fear of not being worthy enough because we are not 'black' or not 'black enough' and are not 'privileged.'

We feel guilt and fear that we will always be tarnished by our history, a history over which we had no control. We were children during Apartheid but recognise that our parents knew and did nothing.

Our fear is manifest in the high walls we build, in the razor wire we twine above the walls and the alarms we set. But more significantly you can see in our eyes our fear and guilt. Its poison infects who we are and how we live our every day.

Our fear is ignited and becomes a vicious cycle as the acts of a few poison our souls. We fear those who plunder possessions, break into houses, assault innocents in the streets or hijack and rape simply because they can, and so turn in on ourselves.

But we long for this to change. We want to be part of an inclusive community. We want to contribute with others. We long to have a place where we can simply grow together in love, each bring our good will, our generosity and our skills to build a resilient rainbow nation.

Some of us have started this work and others wish to use this opportunity to turn dreams into actions.

Already, a couple of us are trying to build better relationships. We believe that by gossiping our stories wherever we can we will extend friendships. One of us is building a Facebook network and has begun having political discussions, which she hopes will lead to finding new ways of generating positive change together. Another is working on a project to bring cheap Internet connectivity into townships so that people can access the world's best and educate themselves at low cost.

These are but a beginning. We wish to extend what we are doing and hope for many more opportunities to find transparent ways of hearing and talking to each other, breaking down prejudice and building together.

Thank you CTT for bringing us together in this way.

I am really taken aback by this contribution. In my three years off the rails, I had been indiscriminate in my choices of victim. Now I heard loud and clear that colour was still an obstacle. How might this affect our view of the outsider and where did Xenophobia begin and end?

I was dragged away from my personal musings as Simon moved us on. "Thank you guys. Now lets move on I think we have just one more group."

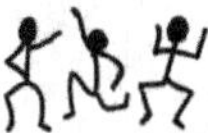

"Our group feels that our work here is too important to celebrate in a dance or a song, so we have chosen to read a statement as our offering to the liturgy."

There were wonderful people who worked with the ANC in the struggle against Apartheid, but now in government we find politicians who believe they are entitled to take the spoils of victory and some who have been convicted of fraud and worse. Within the community, there are collaborators who enjoyed patronage under Apartheid and are still privileged today.

Our government is corrupt and it is the poorest of the poor who depend on the state for resources.

Many who live on the Cape Flats in places like Khayelitsha face massive problems of degradation, isolation, and hopelessness, and for the poorest of the poor hunger and unemployment. Some of these people who are not getting what they hoped are turning to crime, taking drugs and protesting violently.

If we do not begin to take their needs seriously, we may lose the 'rule of law.'

What we see is that the corrupt prosper while the workingman finds it more and more difficult to buy a house in a safe area, to find our way through corruption and patronage, or to live fulfilling lives. It is excruciatingly hard to set this aside but what we bring to this space is a hope that through church, mosque and community we can begin to name racism, regenerate hope and vote for other parties who may begin to move towards governing for all.

What we need to do is actively support honest politicians, the rule of law, the independence of the courts and a free press.

Thank you all for listening.

Simon stands again and begins to speak, but I jump up and ask if I can have a moment. "Sure."

I stretch to fill my whole frame turn to face the sea clap quietly and sing in my deep baritone Nkosi sikelel' iAfrika. Each member stands, takes up the beat and sings with me. There is not a dry face among us. Finally, our hands fall to our sides and we walk out into the sun together. We have begun something new and now need to just be together before we leave.

Our liturgy has run over time so we are asked to move in to a late lunch. We eat quietly. There is little need for words. At the end of our meal Simon stands and almost whispers, "I had a closing statement but now I feel it will take from our experience. Please remember that this is but one step along our path and take care as you leave to focus on your driving. Our experience has been profound and it will be difficult to re-enter the everyday world. Now over to you Nalendi."

Nalendi stands "Um . . . I'm a bit choked up. This has been an extraordinary couple of days. Thank each and every one of you. I also had a closing speech but it doesn't fit any more.

"Themba and I will need to take time to think about how to take our next step forward and I am sure each of you will need to do the same. But please listen to CTT as I am sure I will have plenty to say within a day or two. I will of course contact you all formally within the next month to let you know where to from here. Until then, remember that those people out there have not shared our experience and will live life as if nothing has happened. Look after yourselves and thanks from the bottom of my heart."

Simon stands again. "Now as you leave here please look around and take in our beautiful surroundings, breathe the sea air deep into your lungs, listen to the sounds of this sanctuary, find something to touch and enjoy its texture, and taste this place. Once again, it is very important that you reengage all your senses to bring you back to reality. You each need to do this for your own safety as we have been in a joint meditation and we need to re-enter reality. Thanks and goodbye for now."

TOWARDS FREEDOM

Report back to sponsors

Things have been hectic at CTT since getting back from Monkey Bay. It's been my job to transcribe all the tapes and some brief notes Nalendi took on the weekend. It's wonderful because I get to hear each story, but also exhausting. My computer skills get better each day.

I have phoned everyone to check that they got home OK and to catch their first thoughts after the weekend, and its like chatting with old friends. Everyone is buzzing with ideas about reshaping public opinion and about building more meaningful relationships with those they meet in their daily lives. Sean was so excited "I asked Pieter about looking tired and he told me his kid is in hospital and his wife was crying all the time and . . . I'm listening differently man and they talk about what really matters. It's wonderful!"

Nalendi and I have met for coffee together each morning since the weekend to chat about our project. At first conversations were filled with the wonder and turmoil of the weekend, but now after a week or so we are actually getting down to planning.

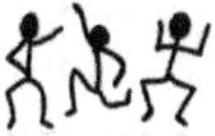

I wake, jump out of bed, reach for my phone and call home. It rings through to voicemail again. "Nomalisa, where are you? Please pick up. OK, I guess you're busy with the twins . . . Monkey Bay was amazing but full on. I've got so much to tell you. Please call." Themba sighs. It's getting harder and harder to be alone.

The trouble is that I feel everything so deeply at the moment. Happy, excited, sad. Its like the world is in my face.

I'm weighed down by the bulk of Table Mountain that looms above the misty haze of morning as I walk to the train. The crush of humanity pushes against me as I jostle to get on the train and isolation bites as I sit hunched over my phone staring at the latest video of the twins tottering around. I wonder if they will recognise me when they see me next. Each emotion is expanded. I feel raw and alive and overwhelmed and I miss my family so much. I want to reach out and grab them, hold them . . . and then my phone is gone. Snatched away. I look up in panic. My lifeline is missing. Where, who took it? "Please, has anyone seen my phone?" The guy beside me laughs. "You must be joking man. It's gone, get over it."

I know this happens every day to someone. But all my numbers, Nomalisa, the twins, my friends, my connection to each one is through my phone. I am devastated. I stagger from the train in tears. I must get a grip. I can't let them see me like this at work. It's just a phone. I push through the door and bump into Nalendi. "What is it? Are you OK?" I shake my head. "My phone was stolen." She smiles. "It's only a phone, Themba!"

"Remember we have the sponsors in today. They want us to take them through the next steps of our project. Hope you have everything ready. You will be reading that story. Hope you've sharpened it. OK see you in ten."

There are five new faces around the table. Coffee is served, an agenda circulated and each person is introduced by title and position. There's that overwhelming shadow. Themba looks around the table very aware of his position. "I'm the ring-in again" he says to himself.

Nalendi starts. "We have decided to begin today's presentation with two stories. We will then take you through the weekend process and offer our thoughts for the way forward before opening up for discussion. OK?" Nods all round. "Themba, over to you."

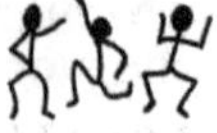

I rub my precious white stone I now carry in my pocket and begin. "Hi, I'm Themba. The vignette I share today has been tweaked and shortened. Names have also been changed. It is about Jacob, who lived on Mitchell's Plain. He is now staying with a friend while he is in rehab for the fourth time."

I'm twenty even if I look older. That's the TIK. I started using when I was fourteen. I joined Badboys 'cos' there was no one home. Soon I was using and my life was over. After that there was only TIK. The last time I went into rehab was after a police shootout at Rocklands. I had a gun and was arrested. People just took justice in their own filthy hands . . . Be vigilant at all times, hey, keep safe. Innocent people die 'cos' they in the wrong places at the wrong times man.

With TIK you feel a rush and your heart hammers like you want to go down on a slag right now, and it goes on and on and yer the hero. Ye'll never forget it cos your heart roars and ye feel mighty, yer invincible.

And then its cool man like yer had some but yer can get more and it don't matter about others cos yer smart and yer tetchy and if yer want something its major so yer just do it cos yer need to and yer don't stop till yer done. And if some slob stops yer, yer just do what yer need to wipe them out so yer can get back to yer thing and if someone gets in the way they're gone and that's it.

Yer don't want to let go of the vibe so yer take more but it's not so good, so yer take still more but it's gone and so are the days man and yer don't remember shit and yer thirst like hell. Yer empty, yer no one, and yer itch like yer got bugs under yer skin and monsters are yelling and yer just want to wipe them out so yer hit or yer shoot or throw stones but nothing works man cos its like yer dead, gone and no one can reach yer.

Then yer back but yer weak as a dog and the only way out is more TIK and if yer can't get any it hurts like hell so yer try to die to quit the pain.

Then there's rehab but yer lost so yer go back to the beginning. Most of the Badboys gang is dead now but maybe yer'l help and give me a chance except I don't know who's there where I used to be, so maybe I'm gone and that's it. I

119

know my name's Jacob and you guy's seem to think there's a God so maybe man. Who knows?

"To be fair this was the most helpless case. Now over to you Nalendi for Selma."

My story is one that has been heard often. My life was always hard but after my mum's removal from District Six to Crossroads on the Flats things got really bad. Mum was one of the lucky ones who still had a job in Cape Town and worked hard. My dad didn't come with us but joined us a couple of years later. This ruined our lives

At first it was just the shouting but then he started telling mum that his second wife was younger and more beautiful. When mum told him to go to her if that was the case he started calling her names and then hitting her. She called the police and he left but then came back on paydays to take her money. When she said no he began hitting again so she called the Imam who talked to dad but that did nothing. He also suggested that mum invite dad's second wife to live with us but mum couldn't do that.

This went on for years before dad hit mum really hard one day and she went into a coma. She died in hospital a while later and dad was sent to jail. He's still there.

My sister and I went to my dad's cousin and stayed there until I married.

I married a Muslim and he now want's to take a second wife. When I said I didn't want this to happen he insisted that he is within his rights and he began to beat me. I have two small children and don't feel I can make it on my own but I'm scared that if I stay things will end the same way for me as they did for my mother.

"When we got back to CTT Themba transcribed all of the stories. We chose the two you heard today because they highlight specific ubiquitous community issues. Other stories were gentler and reflect people's responses to today's political issues. This took all of day one.

"Once each person had been heard, we worked individually to find a pathway towards forgiveness by taking the first steps in acknowledging and letting go of their trauma.

"The following day each small group developed a joint contribution to a ceremony designed to celebrate the healing process.

"In the liturgy we heard each other. We wept, trembled, sang, clung and laughed in concert. Spending the time together telling our stories, naming regrets and beginning to let them go through forgiveness engendered hope.

"The weekend uncovered five themes that underlie South Africa's collective trauma: Displacement and resettlement under Apartheid; government and corporate corruption; family violence and abuse; crime and violence within the community and fear within the community.

"Themba and I suggest three ways forward.

"We suggest twice weekly talkbacks where we bring in a participant, and an expert if appropriate, to share their story and then speak with callers about the issues raised. You all know the old chestnut 'Those who don't learn from history are condemned to repeat it.' In story after story we saw not only the impact of politics on individual lives but also evidence of cycles repeating themselves both within a family unit and carried from one generation to the next.

"These cycles were evident for all five themes. So, in Jacob's case the displacement wrought by Apartheid led to the alienation and absence of his mother, who had to leave early and return late to get to work and her absence led to Jacob's alienation and retreat into addiction. In the case of family violence the daughter is now repeating the pattern created in her mothers life.

"The second idea is that Themba visits participants in the community to document any developments coming out of their healing process, and, lastly, that we use our learnings to help address any issues coming through the news.

"OK, that's us. So over to you for comments and questions."

"I've certainly got one. Your presentations were professional and interesting and the case studies certainly raise importance community issues, but it hasn't answered the question that has been hanging over me since we first decided to go with this project. Is it changing lives and can we expect an impact on our audiences? What we set out to do was change peoples hearts, particularly in relation to xenophobia? Will we achieve this?"

My heart races. Talking about what we heard is one thing but speaking about myself is terrifying. "Come on Themba, you start. You joined the group as a participant." I open my mouth and stutter, "Well, I was hoping to talk professionally but . . ."

My palms are clammy, I can hear the blood rushing through my veins and I'm paralysed. Nothing will come out of my dry mouth and then a hoarse cry comes from the depths of my stomach and everyone sits waiting for my next utterance, which won't come. Nalendi begins to say something but our director holds his hand up to stop her intervention and the silence builds as everyone waits for me.

"I, um . . . the weekend was excruciating, when I heard the story I told I was blown away. I had never given myself a chance to think about my childhood or how much anger and hurt I carried. I was overwhelmed by my fears, and while I have begun to acknowledge my pain and am trying to forgive myself and others there is a long way to go. But if you want to know 'Did the weekend effect me?' More than any other experience in my life. This is very important to me. I believe it is my coming of age experience. I was a lost boy but am now trying to take steps towards being a responsible adult in charge of my life. I will never be the same again.

"Wow . . . and you Nalendi?"

"For me it was like the difference between hearing a weather report and being caught in an electrifying storm. When you await a storm you feel the tightening in your chest as it approaches, the world goes quiet and the sky darkens and then as it hits the rain clatters, the sky shakes with thunder, and lightening rips the heavens apart. I was spellbound by the stories and exhausted by their telling. Being present at the weekend was invigorating, challenging and mind expanding. I will never think about forgiveness or about our country in the same way again.

"How to bring that immediacy to our listeners has been with me every waking moment since coming back and I could not be more excited. This is the biggest challenge I have faced so far in my career and the most important. How do I do justice to . . ."

The sponsor buts in excitedly, "I have a name for the project, *'Without forgiveness we are trapped.'*

Her sidekick chips in "Certainly captures what we hope for, but can we make it a positive imperative maybe 'Forgiveness sets us free'."

"Doesn't emphasise being trapped enough."

"OK. maybe *'Trapped, tell, forgiveness, freedom'*, or *'No future without forgiveness'*."

"That's it *'No future without forgiveness'*. It will remind everyone of the Truth and Reconciliation Commission but we must highlight that this time it is for everyone."

Nalendi takes the visitors to the door, then runs back and throws her arms around me. My arms automatically return the embrace. "They didn't even stop to question us, they loved it. What do think, hey? *No future without forgiveness!* Thanks Themba. It was your reading of Jacob that got them." She kisses me directly on the lips and then leans back into my embrace. "You're terrific."

Bad News

Despite the sponsor's amazing acknowledgement, the news of the day gets in the way of Nalendi's plan to talk on air about *No future without forgiveness*. The talkback lines have been buzzing with yet another issue.

Disappearances happened often but this time a young hiker from Muizenberg was getting more than the usual attention.

This incident is discussed over lunch. Nalendi tells us "His car was found at the end of a road just under Table Mountain and he's vanished. He hasn't returned to his car so a search party is being mustered." A couple of minutes later she suggests "Themba why don't you contact Daniel? He lent a hand fighting the Peninsular fire a month or two ago didn't he? See whether he is up to getting a few people together to help."

Daniel is excited to hear from Themba and immediately suggests, "How about we contact a couple of the Monkey Bay guys to see if they'll join the search."

By evening Themba, Mathue, Daniel, and Brian have volunteered.

The search has been going for a couple of days. It is well organised by people who know the mountain, and it is becoming one of the largest searches ever undertaken in terms of resources and the number of people involved.

Careful planning directs the search so that parties do not cover the same ground twice and searchers work in designated teams. The CTT lot are to stick together and be led by Tom. Weather experts keep a weary eye on the capricious Cape Town conditions.

"If the weather is not conducive to efficient searching then we will have to suspend the search".

We head up the mountain and I am immediately aware of how different the Cape terrain is from the rolling foothills, gushing streams and steep cliff faces of the Drakensburg. Here everything scratches and blocks the path. It is rugged and prickly, inhospitable and beautiful.

Sweat dampens my brow and blocks my vision. I pant and curse under my breath as I trudge behind Daniel up a steep ravine. We can't spread out here because there is only this small break between sandstone cliffs. I can't go another step and yet I must. "What am I doing here? I'm just not fit enough."

Tom leads our team of five as we scour our small part of the mountain. He is strict, direct and careful and we follow each instruction without question. He is the expert and trained to manage himself and our welfare as well as the search. He makes sure we keep together, eat small snacks consistently, keep hydrated, rest regularly and always stay within easy earshot.

At the end of each day we collapse exhausted from trudging through Cape scrub, scrambling up sheer rock faces and through deep slippery-sided kloofs but we never feel unsafe or in danger ourselves. We learn discipline in even the smallest minutiae, like how to examine an extinguished campfire "Probably set by a Bergie." We also appreciate being part of a larger whole who are kept informed about all aspects of the search.

We know we are not working alone. Search and Rescue Police with their helicopters and the dog squad lead the operation. We are treated well as an important auxiliary force.

We are too tired to talk about our experience on the mountain but appreciate being part of something significant. People from all over the Cape are following the search on CTT and we particularly like that they are phoning in to wish us well in our search.

By the end of day four the search command is concerned that parties have scoured the mountains from Devil's Peak, and the Twelve Apostles through Orange Kloof in Hout Bay and out as far as Silvermine but all without success, so they review all possible scenarios.

Our small team works together from morning until evening for four days but like the others we are unsuccessful in our task.

We are exhausted and raw and try to hide our loss of hope from each other. Our time together, even when we are not searching, is consumed with what we might have missed, where we should look again, how to be more careful, and how we will keep others hoping when ours is fading fast.

But something else had happened to us over this time. We have become firm friends, each understanding the others in a new way. We now know what specific skills each has, when to speak and when to be quiet. We also know that facing a difficult task together is better than facing it alone.

On day five other canine units are also deployed to assist the Cape Town Police's dog unit who have been searching since day one and more people are involved. By Saturday close to a hundred searchers are deployed and more than forty people resume the search on Sunday. On Monday search command decide that our missing mountaineer would not be found. "Something else must have happened. Either he has been killed or abducted. The search may continue but from now on it will become a police matter." All volunteer searchers are dismissed.

The final debriefing is professional with each of us taken through our positive contribution and reminded of the emotional toll such work will have on us all. "Remember to get good rest, feed yourselves well and to talk to each other or the professional debriefers if necessary." We are warned "You may suffer from survivor guilt, from concerns that you could have done more and possibly an ongoing anxiety that our world is not safe.

"Be gentle on yourselves, remember that you have done well and think long and hard about the positives you have learned about yourself and those who worked alongside you. Thank you for your service to our community."

Mathue, Daniel, Brian and I wave Tom goodbye and go off for a beer. We sit together quietly for half an hour and then leave, all strong in the knowledge we now trust each other without thinking. These are my new Impi brothers. Daniel invites me to stay the night and suggests that I phone Nomalisa and bring her up to date on what we have been doing.

I am engulfed in panic. For five days I have forgotten that my phone was stolen and I don't know Nomalisa's number. What will I do?

Daniel wakes me next morning. "Sorry to wake you but you have a call."

"What?" I take the phone . . . "Hallo Themba here."

"Hi Themba, it's Nalendi and you are through to CTT mornings. I am in the studio with Roberto who has been telling us his story and taking calls on homelessness. We have had a couple of queries about how you guys are after your days on the mountain so we have called to ask you."

"Oh . . . fine I guess . . . but exhausted, and sad that we were unsuccessful. Sorry that I'm not in this morning . . . I . . . well I guess I overslept. We are all a little exhausted, but well. Working together on the mountain was hard and unfortunately, as you know, we came back empty handed. But toiling together on a worthwhile task has been life affirming. Again, Nalendi, forgive me. I will be in as soon as I can pull myself together."

"Ah, but you are here with our listeners right now, on air. We are all with you Themba, and by the way your wife and twins are doing fine and very proud of their dad and looking forward to hearing from you soon."

Just as I'm about to reply Roberto chips in "give our best to the CTT volunteers man. We are proud of you and now turn on your radio man and listen and remember God is watching hey."

"Thanks Themba. We wanted you all to know that CTT was informed about what you were part of each day and many callers have had contact with us wishing you well. With you, our four, out there we all felt we were part of the search and we ache with you guys. You are our heroes! OK mate, have a restful day. We need to get back to our callers now. See you in here tomorrow."

Daniel smiles and turns the radio up loud, and here is Roberto relaxed and fielding a call. Daniel's son comes in with a cup of tea and a wide grin. "You are my hero too dude. I put three sugars in your tea. Is that OK?"

"Thanks" I ruffle his hair and turn my attention to the radio.

"Yes Nalendi, I am living in a garage in Fish Hoek at the moment and looking after a couple of dogs while the lady is away with family in Joburg. It's starting to cool right down at night now and the bridge at the harbour isn't safe any more since our stuff was burned. Also, once the tourist season is over there is less food. We get the left overs from a restaurant in Main Street in season, but in winter people stay home out of the weather. I still come to the harbour once a week to meet my regulars who need their medication but mostly we look for shelter. Even the Bergies try to find some relief from the wet and cold. There are a couple of caves on the mountain but some of them choose to stay at a shelter in Kalk Bay through the winter."

Now Nalendi invites callers to join the conversation. Beth is first. "So is homelessness a choice then?"

"No Mam. You know there is a housing crisis. Otherwise we wouldn't have places like Khayelitsha and I wouldn't live rough. Especially as it is getting more and more dangerous with all the foreigners. It doesn't matter whether they come from PE or Zim, they are flooding the Cape and making it harder for us. There's much less room, more squatter camps and less to go round and when people are hungry they steal.

Even from people like me who never steals on principle. This makes us all unsafe and Xenophobia grows. Rastafarians don't steal and we don't drink but we do use the weed and our God watches over us man.

"I believe that God has made enough for all of us under the sun but life is dangerous, especially for homeless women. People like my girlfriend Ruth are very scared and depressed man because for them there is less safety with family violence, and violence and rape in the community. Life is very hard on the street man and it is getting harder every year."

"So why don't you get work?"

"I get work where I can and my selling to those who need weed to manage their pain is also work. You may not see it that way but many do. I like to pay my own way. I also do dog walking for families who work during the week, Mam, but I say to you there are many people and few jobs. Unemployment is huge and I think you know that."

"I guess you are right Roberto and I'm sorry if I seemed disrespectful but there are many of us who are scared of people like you."

"No need man. Rastafarians are peace loving people. I will pray for you. God bless."

"OK, thanks Beth. Now over to you, Peter."

"Hi. Johan here not Peter, I am in town planning and I feel I need to bring some realism into this discussion. I want to remind your listeners that we cannot talk about homelessness without first mentioning the unemployment level, which is almost 35% in South Africa and youth unemployment is over 44%. It is no wonder that with this number of people out of work we have such vast housing problems here. It is estimated that we need to build over three million houses if we are to offer housing to all. But this isn't all. As you know there are also problems with the housing now available.

"Most townships and squatter settlements lack the basic infrastructure and services of water, sewerage, and electricity.

Efforts to solve this must focus not only on construction, but also on servicing current and prospective sites by building roads and providing electricity, sanitation, and water. An estimated 66% of the country's population have no access to electricity, and in most black townships there is only one water tap to service several thousand people."

"Thanks for that reminder, Johan. Now we have Samuel wanting to respond specifically to the issues you raise."

"Ya, Johan makes it all sound like facts and I want you to know what it's really like. I live in Khayelitsha and its hell. When you put Johan's bloody bullshit into real words. I rent a tin lean-to, tacked onto an outhouse on a mud track behind a high wall next to the railway line. I have space for a bed and a box to hold my clothes. I get light from a wire that my landlord has tacked onto the mains so he can steal it from the electricity supply that runs outside his government built house, and I have to walk at least one hundred meters to the nearest water. The long drop toilet, if you can call it that, is another twenty meters away and stinks so much that I hate using it. About one hundred people go there. For this wonderful hellhole I have to pay him each week or he will throw me out, but he doesn't pay his rent or electricity. Sometimes I think of reporting him but I'm too scared he will get someone to kill me if I do. That's the housing problem and that's why people like Roberto are homeless. Not so, hey?"

"You are right bro. The housing out your way is bad. Ever tried straight under God's stars? It's OK when the weather is good. You tell the truth, it is bad out there and when you add the gangs it's no place on God's earth for anyone. But for me there is God and he cares about the birds of the air who do not sow or reap. This brings me hope for you and me and our future."

"OK, thanks Samuel." Nalendi says, "I know there's so much more we need to discuss. Brave of you to tell it like it is. I wish we could continue, and thank you so much Roberto. There's still so much we could talk about and many callers waiting, who I am afraid we will have to disappoint for today.

We are already well over time. Please remember that. No future without forgiveness is now a twice-weekly segment, and on Thursday we will hear from our own Themba. So please tune in. Now to the news headlines. Sorry to have kept you waiting John."

Over a very late breakfast, Daniel, Marie, his wife, and I chat about how well Roberto handled callers. Marie comments that this is the first time she has heard someone who is homeless speak so clearly about his difficulties. "It's wonderful that your project can highlight this issue in such a personal way and Roberto certainly challenged the medical community about using Dagga as medication."

Then the conversation shifts to my family and my hopes to bring them to Cape Town as soon as my job becomes permanent and I find suitable housing. I'm beginning to love the area between Kommetjie and Fish Hoek and Daniel says that there are some reasonable rentals that come up from time to time. He offers to help me look once I'm ready.

After breakfast he asks whether I would like to speak to Nomalisa, says, "don't worry" to my mumbles about Nomalisa's lost number and sits me down at a computer and dials. Nalendi has found the number in my staff records. "This will cost me nothing so speak for as long as you like."

Nomalisa's voice is clear and full. It is wonderful to finally speak. I have so much I want to talk about but first she put's the twin's on and I am blown away. Their voices are different and I can't tell them apart. They each say Tata and then babble away in a language known only to them. I am missing so much. My voice chokes as I ask how they are. I want to be with them now and am overwhelmed with pride and longing.

Nomalisa takes back the phone, "My hero! we have been following your exploits on the radio. What was it like to search for days?"

Talking to Nomalisa I open myself up to all my fears and longings of the last weeks. "I am different my love, For the first time I have allowed myself to look at all the anger and pain you have seen within me. I now understand what you meant when you talked about the importance of losing a father. I see the links between this loss and my need to be in control and I am so sorry that I pushed you away so often. Thank you for your patience. I miss you so." I go on to talk about my weekend away and the time on the mountain and Nomalisa says, "I am pretty exhausted too with the twins and work and housework and no life outside. Your mother is getting old and thinking of going back to her village but loves the twins so stays on in Saxonwold when she should retire. You know there is more street violence in Soweto than previously. It's getting more and more dangerous."

"I am sorry you are there on your own Nomalisa."

"Ya, Themba! This is not a place to raise children. Especially without their father. And now there is even talk that the water will be restricted or even cut off for a couple of days. It is hard to live like this."

We chat as if we are together in the same room and perhaps an hour later she asks "Have you any idea when we will be able to join you?"

"I am still on probation my love, but am saving. I cannot promise anything yet."

"Don't leave it too long. The twins will not know you and I do not like living alone. I need a husband."

Themba

Nalendi hugs me as she enters the CTT office. I flush. "Great to have you back Themba. Lots to talk about. I know you're on the phones this morning but can we meet after lunch for an hour or so?"

Calls for the rest of the morning are peppered with people specifically phoning to welcome me back and thank me for representing them on the search. I have become their proxy.

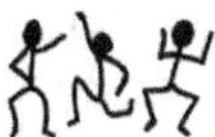

It's Thursday morning and I'm on air. But before I begin my story Nalendi reminds people that today's program is another in the series No future without forgiveness and invites listeners to keep in mind how they can contribute towards a more inclusive community.

I tell my story and am again surprised by the intensity and fervour with which I speak. I am nervous and this ups the vehemence of my narrative. I spend some time talking about Monkey Bay and when I talk about watching my crumpled paper burn I gasp and swallow. My palms are wet, my tongue dry. "I wish I had known my father!" I whisper to the world. "How can I be a man when he was not there to teach me?" Then I sit dumbstruck for what seams to be a lifetime. Nalendi does not fill the hanging silence.

Then Akani is put through and talkback begins. "Your story is powerful, Themba, thank you for letting us see your other side. I saw a photo of you and your team on the mountain. You went well on the rescue my brother. Working shoulder to shoulder with a team must be good. It builds trust, ya?"

"Ya and it was especially amazing to be invited to stay in a white home while we were volunteering. I realise I am still a black man at heart because I was so surprised to be included in their family life without question." To myself I think I like

Mathue, Daniel and Brian but can I truly trust them in a tight corner? I'm still not completely sure.

Akani continues, "You know, Themba, you are among the lucky ones. You knew your father for a while and you got to see your mother during school holidays. And now she is there to help with her grandchildren. This is wonderful. There are many of us who grew up only with our grandmothers. Because of AIDS we have never known either parent."

Themba answers "This is true my friend." But inside myself I do not see the big strong black man on the mountain but rather the harassed child in a token job who is full of confusion, anger, helplessness and an immense loneliness. I am so confused. Change and taking responsibility is easy enough to talk about but to act on? That is almost inconceivable.

I felt at one with others at Monkey Bay and on the mountain, but here and now I vacillate, I am weary. No. In fact right now I am down right scared. I heard from a couple of coloured fellas that they struggle with who they are but I am torn apart right now, so how do I embrace this 'orphan' and the caller, and show sympathy?

Nalendi sees my distress and fills for me. "Yes, Akani, Themba did know his parents and AIDS is still a scourge on our country, and hopefully we will be able to find time to discuss this as a separate issue. It is certainly one we need to think about. But for now we have a full board of callers. Thank you and keep listening and please keep on keeping us honest."

The next person to speak is a voice from the past, an Impi brother. He speaks first in Zulu but Nalendi asks him to speak English so that all listeners can understand what he is saying.

"You are no longer my brother, Themba, you are a sell out. A Zulu does not show his emotion to the world. We check our strength and our pain. We do not share it with others. What are you doing talking to the world? Is this work? You should be standing shoulder to shoulder with your brothers in the mines. Especially now when we don't earn enough to feed our families and are fighting for better wages. Who are you? You are not the Themba I knew. Shame on you man."

I reach into my pocket and touch my white pebble. I need grounding.

Nalendi talks into my silence. "Dumisani, I hear you are angry but have you not been listening. It was only yesterday that we spoke about the miners' strike. Or perhaps you do not usually listen to our program. We are with you brother! Every worker deserves a fair days pay for his work. Now do you have anything further to say because there are many other callers waiting?"

"No, and thank you for your support Nalendi but no thanks to you Themba. You are white bread, a coconut, not the boy warrior who became a man alongside me. Goodbye and we can speak about your betrayal, off air perhaps?"

I grit my teeth. What does Dumisani know of my life? I saw him last at fourteen. And yet he's right. I no longer stand solidly with the Zulu belief that the ANC works for the empowerment of its people. I am a doubter. Oh shit, I am so confused.

What does our 'disciplined force of the left', the ANC, show after twenty-one years in power? Corruption is everywhere and everything is falling apart and all the government does is give excuses and cover up its inadequacies. There are some among them who are now multimillionaires while their people are dirt poor. And then there are the many issues they simply ignore. When I first saw headlines like 'Dozens killed in South Africa mine shooting' I thought it was referring back to the Apartheid era. But Marikana happened on their watch. They have betrayed us, and I for one no longer trust them. I now have new aspirations for our country. I love the Democratic Alliance's dream of one nation built on freedom, fairness and opportunity for all. Is this being a coconut . . . well? Then, perhaps I am one.

A caller interrupts Themba's thoughts. "I'm Sello and this is the first time I'm brave enough to phone the radio but I have too much to say to you to be scared."

"Welcome, Sello I am here to talk."

"I need to say being a good person is like being a goalkeeper, no matter how many goals you save, people will only remember the ones you missed."

"OK I hear you man."

Sello continues, "Opportunity is missed by most people because it is dressed in overalls and looks like work. There is a race that you must run, so go for it brother. You know for me this world is not home, it's like an animal farm . . . but even though it's hard, my dear God will always carry me over."

Nalendi joins in. "Hi Sello. It sounds like you have done it tough. Can you tell us a little about yourself."

"I went up to matric. That was last year before university. I'm forty-one, married with one baby girl and presently expecting a baby boy in September this year. My home language is Southern Sotho. I have never had anything good happen to me as I have been struggling since my childhood but I hope good things are coming, hey. For the past four years I have struggled so bad cause I took my wife to university. She just completed her diploma in Logistics and I hope she finds a job as soon as possible so I can take a short course too, hey."

Themba asks, "Do you have work Sello? There are so many of us who just can't find any with unemployment so high."

"I'm a farm caretaker at an animal farm here in the Eastern Cape. And must say we are just a little happy family, except we can't meet the challenges financially. I'm really pulling hard even though we never go to bed hungry."

"Sounds hard, Sello. Do you have anything you want to say about your struggles?"

"Yes I do. I believe in Jesus but still I am not happy with our government. So many things have been going wrong like electricity with load shedding all the time and Marikana and Nkandla. Zuma is a bad man to take our money when so many of us struggle even to eat and live."

"OK and . . ."

"As far as politics go I am not so happy with the ANC, even though they are a black government. With Madiba gone they forget us. I think Maimane is a good man. I like that guy because he isn't afraid to speak his mind. I really don't know much about him, except he is on the good side. He is a pastor, so I only know him as a spiritual father hey, but I am praying that he will help us."

"So economics are important to you, Sello?"

"Yes God is interested in our work. Whether you are a truck driver, a school crossing guard, a physicist, or a physician your job is a way to reflect the glory of God. So economics is important."

"Thanks Sello. Its great to know that you listen to us, and God bless you. Is there anything further you wish to say to Themba?"

"No just keep speaking because its good to hear real life over the radio and it gives people like me hope hey. Thank you."

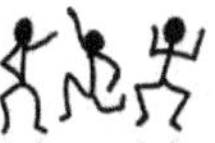

The next caller has waited a while and jumps straight in. "I want to add my impressions of Mmusi Maimane. After going to hear him in the flesh three times, he does impress me. He's very well spoken, hardly ever refers to notes and is definitely charismatic but not a pushover. When one hears him in Parliament, he comes across quite forceful. He is very passionate about South Africa and I certainly hope he is correct when he says the DA is making inroads amongst the urban black community. The municipal elections next year will give us a better idea. He is still fairly new in the job and untried, but hopefully he has some seasoned campaigners backing him. Helen Zille certainly gave him her support in the leadership election and I respect her judgement."

Themba responds, "That was very clear thank you."

"Unfortunately the ANC of today does not have the leaders of integrity we would have liked . . . Mandela must be turning in his grave!"

"Thanks for that, and I think we can fit in just one more caller."

"Hi and thanks for taking my call. Well! Mmusi Maimane is a very well spoken intelligent young man that seems to deeply care about the country and its people. His challenge in my mind is to grow the DA into the black voter base without estranging the white voters. This is going to be hard because the interests of both groups in reality stand in competition to each other. So how he's going to lead in such a way that no one loses? That is the question."

"Thanks that was to the point so perhaps just one last call. Johan, you are on. Please make it quick."

"Not sure I can, but here goes. For me the issue is that everything is decided outside of parliament now in the party room. This is not democratic. Also with no constituency representation people have no local member to take issues to.

"Politicians will only listen and help when their jobs depend on it.

"No sign of parliament looking at what people want what with Marikana, Zuma's house, housing problems, electricity, and in parliament there is no follow through. The ANC needs to be thrown out. Maimane seems to want an active democracy working with people, so lets throw our support behind him. I think that's me for now. Thanks."

"OK a difficult one to end with. but again I ask what has today taught us about No future without forgiveness? Clearly we can't just forgive and forget. We as a society must find ways to hold our politicians accountable, and I guess it is at the ballot box that we do this. So how, if at all, will today's discussion contribute towards influencing the way you vote? That is all for today, but we will be back with more on Tuesday. Thanks Themba and you listeners out there. Thanks for listening and thanks for your calls."

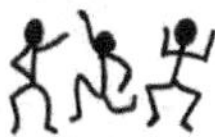

Nalendi and Themba walk from the studio together. "Well! I didn't expect the morning to become so political. I guess everything is political when half the population are close to or below the poverty line. How was it to be confronted by your Impi brother?"

"Challenging."

"Do you want to talk?"

"Yes. I am feeling very mixed up. There is so much going through my head. I am full of feelings of power and strength after the rescue. Being part of a working physical team has put me very much in touch with my masculinity and my strength. It is good to have depended on my body and on working with others to achieve a physical task. But on the other hand the stuff that Dumisani said is right. I question myself about being a sell out, a 'good kaffir' working in a white man's rescue. My brothers would have done the same thing very differently.

"Then there is also another side to me that I am shy to share because perhaps it is presumptuous to do so with you when I am not yet sure of myself and you are to all intents and purposes my boss. Getting some small recognition through the work we have done is building a desire to do more than report what is happening in the world. I am aware of the beginnings of a flame of passion to lead men and become more active in politics. It is not enough to report on corruption. Now that I have voiced publicly that I am no longer a loyal ANC man, I want to help shape the way we think about politics and what we do to change things."

"Oh tell me more Mr Themba please."

"Don't tease. That guy who started the thing at Cape Town University about the Rhodes statue. I didn't like the way he did it but he certainly is contributing to changing public opinion and is inspiring people to act. I want that, I think."

"Wow. How different you have become in the four and half months since we first met, and I must say I like what I see. Now how about using these ambitions to help shape our programs. We are getting more and more calls and the program's exciting lots of people, but it's not going smoothly in the direction we had planned.

"I guess we were naive to think that callers wouldn't want to include the whole gamut of South Africa's woes, but we do want people to look at the link between getting to understand our pain and struggles and Xenophobia. So what do we do differently with our approach."

"Nalendi, sorry but I think you are wrong we are doing exactly what we had hoped by getting callers to identify with the stories presented. What I think we have to focus on is how to begin asking people about their mistakes and pain and ask them to think about how this gets in the way of their living fulfilled lives in our unique South African situation.

"You know what keeps coming to mind for me is that it is exactly as Jesus said. People can only be saved from themselves one at a time and this will only come as they deal with their problems and set themselves free."

"A bit too much like an evangelist for me Themba but I get your drift."

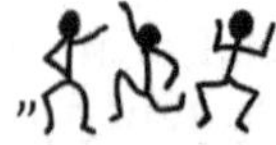

That night on the train I think again about my outspoken comments to Nalendi. Do I believe in Jesus or is it just that being around people that talk about God rubs off? I certainly am in a continual spiral about forgiveness. If I can really let go of my anger at losing my dad and mum and about being in a country where I can only chase my dreams by leaving my wife and kids at such a crucial time in their lives, what will fill the gap? Can I believe in myself? Can I become a firebrand? can I lead men?

Well, I can dream. And right now I know that the 'Healing of Memories' is right about one thing. One cannot step forward with confidence until one feels right in oneself, and for me this cannot happen until I have let my past go.

When I get home to my cold room, I shower and go to bed without dinner. Later I wrestle with wild dreams. I am lost on the mountain when I am grabbed from behind by a tall angry bear of a man, who holds me around the neck while I thrash helplessly to free myself. Each time I try to wrestle free I entangle myself more.

As I thrash I am unable to scream as my tongue thickens. My captor laughs in a deep resonant base. It grows louder but more muffled as I become aware of the blood gushing through my hammering heart. The mountain mist creeps closer. It seeps into my lashing limbs and I am overwhelmed by the sour taste of my reaching stomach as I begin to choke myself on my own vomit.

My captor does nothing but hold me in giant grip and laugh.

I see Daniel. He looks in my direction from close by, but does not see or hear my writhing body dangling just a meter away. "My God where is he? He was just ahead a minute ago and now he's gone. Themba . . . !"

I go cold and my writhing stops. The bear of a man lets go and I slip to the ground cold and damp and clammy. "God save me!"

Now I calm myself. Breathe more evenly again and call to out to God. But I can't see him. Instead I see Nalendi smile mischievously at me. She crooks her little finger and says in a gentle sultry voice

"Themba come here. It's God or me and I'm closer."

Soda

The wind cuts through my beanie and my ears throb with cold as I face into the wind and head up Whale Street towards the Bo-Kaap museum. I hope Soda has somewhere warm in mind because the rain is almost horizontal and this biting wind could carry us all the way to Bloubergstrand. Nobody warned me about the Cape winter. It eats into my bones and I can't believe it is only two weeks since we wandered around Monkey Bay in our shirtsleeves.

I hear Soda's loud curse as I dash across Buitengracht Street and am almost clipped by a car I haven't seen through the rain. "Hey I just got a friend don't go killing him off man!" He grabs my arm and drags me up the hill, up some steps and in through glass doors. "Welcome to my parlour sir." To a man behind a counter he says, "This is the important guest I spoke about. Say hallo to Mr Themba from CTT and then the movie please." The attendant greets me, we go through a door and take a seat, I pant and the bioscope begins.

The movie is black and white and grainy. Two women in their sixties walk along an empty street in rubble filled District Six with Table Mountain in the background. Their voices are choked as they talk about the homes they have lost and the family and friends who disappeared to somewhere on the Cape Flats never to be seen again. Our Monkey Bay stories jump alive again; the anger, the hopelessness, the trauma. "That small one was my aunty" says Soda "she died of a broken heart."

But then the film shifts to talk about Harold Cressy, a head teacher at a co-educational school, Trafalgar Second Class Public School. He was the first coloured person to gain a degree, a Bachelor of Arts, in South Africa. When the Apartheid government tried to move the school, the staff refused to be moved. By 1982, 60,000 people had been moved out of the area and re-housed on the Cape Flats. This meant that many students had to be transported in to the school but despite this, they still achieved high pass rates. My heart leaps, Nalendi and I are struggling with how to pitch some aspects coming out of our time away in a positive political frame. And here is one of the themes highlighted at Monkey Bay, easily accessible, with hope grounded in its history. Warren is our example of education as hope and positive resistance, and Daniel with his Internet work is our trailblazer. Now we can link it with work from before the removals.

"OK man, on your feet, now I'm taking you on an inside walk through Bo-Kaap so you don't freeze your bum off." We go out a back door up some steel steps and into an upper hall. Along one wall, a multi coloured Bo-Kaap shouts "look at me" and Soda dances in front of the mural pointing out his special places. "This was my Ouma's house, this where I went to school and this, my man, is the Mosque where we used to fight. We loved taunting the imam and then running for our lives. I've basically lived in this place for all my life man, so any questions before I take you on the outside."

By the time we leave the museum the rain has stopped, the wind has dropped slightly and the brightly painted multi coloured walls sparkle in the sun. Each house is painted a different rainbow colour. Soda points up to the left, beyond a wrought iron gate, at a newly paved path. "Remember Fazel, who was in jail for nine years? Well this here is his handiwork. Good pointing hey? The guy he worked for is a bastard. Only paid him half what he owed. And up this street, see the building work site on the right, that white creep builder is ruining the neighbourhood. He keeps talking about the gangs who steal from the tourists. Doesn't he know that the 'skollies' add to the Bo-Kaap vibe? That old house belonged to a friend and we used to play poker every Friday, but the area got gentrified so he couldn't afford to live there any more. Now we're going to have a swanky white woman who is into art and inner city living. No way they're going to turn us lot into gents!"

We round a corner, pass a mosque and stop outside a store with a large Coca Cola sign painted on one wall. "Come on into my office man. It's out of the cold." He walks in past an iron grill and says "Hey hallo Mohamed this is my man. Themba, Mohamed from Somalia. He's our local Xeno . . . So, Mr North Africa, tell Themba about your family. It's for his program on CTT man.

"Oh., OK. Good afternoon Themba, I like the sound of what you are doing. Thank you! Do you want me to talk?"

"Sure thank you."

"I've been in Cape Town for a few of years, now but I came to Durban when we first fled. You know we Somalis are known as businessmen, so when I had to escape for my life from the flying bullets on the streets of Mogadishu I followed my uncle and began helping in his shop. I was lucky I had somewhere to run. But then in 2008 his shop was burned down and he ran away so I came to Cape Town because that seemed safer."

"Why?"

"Because I read in the paper that in Cape Town there were also riots in 2008 but in Masiphumelele, a squatter settlement on the Cape Peninsular, the community leaders helped refugees who had run from the violence to return. They also got the broader community to apologies to the shop owners, mostly Somali's like me, and ensured that goods stolen from our shops were returned. Every newspaper headlined Masi and I was so excited that I came here."

"First I helped run a small street store in Masi and then I heard about this shop in Bo-Kaap and came to help here. When the owner went back to Mogadishu I stayed on and I have bought the shop myself now. I am accepted here, attend the local mosque and intend to marry and bring my wife to Bo-Kaap. The only problem is that visa's are so difficult."

"Where did you meet your girl, Mohamed?"

"She and I were betrothed many years ago, before I fled. But my uncle has made the arrangements. That is how we do it where I come from."

"Well I know how difficult it is to be separated. My wife and twins are in Johannesburg and I can't wait to get them here, so good luck man. Hope that visa gets sorted soon."

Soda smiles at me, "He's my no good Muslim Xeno, Themba. You better get your own. Now I want to take you for the best samosa in Cape Town so get moving man."

We say our goodbyes and head further up the hill into the biting wind. When we get to the shop, Soda insists on going in so I chat to young man outside. He is twenty-three, a sports teacher who took two years to find a job and is now saving madly to go overseas and look for a football scholarship. He says he wants to get out of this hopeless country. I smile "I want to change it."

Soda comes out of the shop laughing. "I didn't mean you have to pick up just any old trash, man. Hey, Jannie, you still heading for glory in the US? Don't you go corrupting this guy! He's my friend and I need him here . . . OK Themba the first up to the firing range gets the coke. Let's go." He dashes up the hill and I follow panting. We stop half way up Lions Head at the old gun range, snug in next to a canon barrel, shiver just a little, eat delicious samosas and stare out across Cape Town docks and the World Cup Soccer Stadium, and out across the bay to Bloubergstrand. I pull out my white pebble and hold it up for Soda to see. He reaches into his pocket and brings his out. We smile at each other and Soda says, "Snap."

What a view! This is God's own country and it is wonderful to be enjoying it with a friend.

Family Violence

"Good morning folks, here we are again talking about No future without forgiveness. As you know CTT has run several programs addressing family violence because it is such an overwhelming problem within most if not all communities. Well, today we have both Ayesha and Ali on together. They have specifically asked for this as they began talking together at Monkey Bay about issues Ayesha had in her marriage. Ayesha has taken it upon herself to raise awareness of family violence in her community and particularly about what happens in many cases where a man marries a second wife within the Muslim faith. Ali, who is on an elders council within his region, has agreed to join this discussion today."

Ali begins with a brief reflection on his life.

I came from a Muslim family which has faced ostracism from the community at large and our opportunities have always been restricted.

We were removed from District Six to Athlone under Apartheid and this disrupted our lives greatly. My parents were poor but they worked hard to educate all five children and as the the eldest son I looked after mum after dad died.

When I married my wife and I decided that she would not work. She was a housewife and was home to help the children when they faced the difficulties wrought on us by the Apartheid Government. So when the caspers came into my son's school she was there to comfort him when he ran home in fright.

I believe my children all took the right pathways because their mother was always there for them. So while children from other families became drug aditcts mine all took the right path, thanks be to Allah.

Our family has always been a part of the Muslim community, and I have respect within my community. I am a trustee of seven mosques. As a Muslim I believe my destiny is in His hands and while I know that you must tether the camel to keep it from roaming, my life is in the hands of Allah. We are given our life and must make the most of it.

"Thanks Ali, Ayesha we will hear from you before we invite callers to join us."

Ayesha talks only about how she became a Muslim and married into her new faith. She focuses on the effect of her husband taking a second wife and only telling her once it was a *"fait accompli."* She then engages Ali saying, "I have many friends who have found themselves in similar situations. I have tried to engage with imams on the issues of family violence, which I believe is almost sanctioned by the Muslim faith. Also it is my experience that quite often men take a second wife without consulting their first. Several Muslim women I know have had no option but to flee their marriage for their lives."

"OK callers over to you, what would you like to ask either Ayesha or Ali or add to our conversation."

The first caller, Mary, asks to speak directly to Ali. "Before we begin discussing this topic I need to ask what you believe about women. Clearly your religion subjugates women. Where do you personally stand on the issue of women's rights?"

"I have learned from Islam that men and women are different but equal and I am certain there is no authority in the Qur'an for the type of regular and frequent acts of violence that women in our community often experience from their husbands. However I know you are right. There are Moslems who do not agree with my interpretation."

"OK, well then, what are you going to do about those creeps who keep their women at home and out of sight? I have heard that the reason your women wear burkas and long dresses is to hide the bruises. The holier than though responses from the imams do not fool me. Who are you protecting? I am sure it's the so called men and their pride rather than their wives virtue."

"Well I am not sure how to respond to those comments. I believe we see extreme behaviours from all religions and by the way my wife wears neither a burka or especially long dresses. She usually wears trousers."

"Ah yes you would say that but we are discussing the evils of Islam today."

"Mary, this is Ayesha and I'm sorry but I'm not sure how your haranguing Ali will help. I want you to know that I have spent some time talking with him and he genuinely wants to find a way to help with the problem I have raised."

"Well! I don't want to sound sceptical but I won't hold my breath, but good for you. Keep trying. Just know that I have raised these issues for many years with no success."

"Thank you Mary." Nalendi immediately takes the next call.

"Hi my name is Samira and I work at a Muslim woman's health clinic. Congratulations for opening up this very difficult issue. I'm sorry but I must say that my experience supports Mary's comments. I have been helping Muslim women escape domestic violence for fifteen years now and the problem is huge. So many women have been left destitute and barely alive. They have been subjugated by religious leaders who use a misogynistic interpretation of the Qur'an to entrench male power."

"Yes Samira that is exactly our point. We very much want to challenge this entrenched misogamy in Muslim Communities."

"Well Ali, at least we have begun. Previously Muslim marriage was not recognised under South African law so Muslim woman had no protection at all and nowhere to turn but finally in 2014, several imams were accredited as marriage officers under the 1961 Marriage Act. So now Muslim couples can be married by imams from within your religion but with full legal status and with that they are afforded the same protections of any civil marriage."

"Thanks for bringing that to our attention Samira. At present, unfortunately, this is only known in the more enlightened communities. At the moment Ayesha and I are planning a series of talks to the imams in my region. We hope to have our first meeting next month at a joint forum in Athlone. This will be one fact we will highlight in those meetings."

"Fantastic. I applaud your work but in the meantime I would like to provide a number to any woman listening who needs help.

"Listeners, if your husband is violent make contact with us as soon as you can. Don't wait until it's too late. Remember that abusive and violent behaviour comes in cycles so please be vigilant. Usually after a particularly bad outburst the perpetrator is overcome with regret and promises to do anything to win back your trust. This will often lead to an almost honeymoon period where he will woo you back with generosity and love but with time this heralds another build-up and explosion of anger. These cycles get shorter and tighter and unfortunately many women die or get close to death because they don't recognise these warnings or act quickly enough. So please phone now and together we will immediately develop a personal safety plan and go from there. Also to you men who are listening, recognise that what I am saying is true for you and if you want to change your behaviour phone and we'll direct you to a man who will help."

"Samira, Ayesha here. I wish I had heard your explanations of the violence cycle sooner. It may have saved me a great deal of grief. Now back to our initiative of speaking to imams, could you contribute to our forums?"

"I would love to. Call me after the talkback and we can make plans. I would love to be involved and thanks so much for addressing this very difficult topic."

Nalendi speaks "Thank you Samira. OK. Hi Mohamed, you are on air now."

"I am incensed! Keep out of our business. This country fought long and hard for the recognition of all people and religions and here we have you telling us how to live our lives again. This is not a public issue."

Ayesha stands angrily to deliver her reply unaware for a moment that she cannot be seen. "Mohamed you are talking with fellow Muslims here today, and hiding family violence behind religion is exactly what we are on about. It is attitudes like yours that entrench the problem."

"I must support Ayesha. Mohamed, when men use Allah's name to condone their behaviour they sin against Him and his people. We must call violence in any form for what it is. I will pray for you my brother and I ask you to go to your imam, tell him what you have heard today and ask him to join the conversation also."

Mohamed hangs up.

Another call is put through but only a whisper is heard. "I need help. My husband beats both me and his first wife. What can we do?"

Ayesha is immediately alert. "Are you safe at the moment?"

"Yes."

"Hold on one second and we will take your number off air and get someone to call you back directly. Thank you for taking the risk to call. We are with you my sister."

Nalendi supports Ayesha. "It's great that someone is willing to seek help and I believe the phones are now overwhelmed with calls so if you are phoning because you need help here is Lifelines number. It is open twenty-four hours a day and they are specifically trained in this area."

Another caller comes on air. "This is Sheik Ishmael and I wish to address the issue of marriage. The Qur'an allows for a man to take four wives."

Ali responds. "It does Sheik, but the Qur'an also says that a man is responsible for the maintenance of his wife or wives. If a man has more than one wife, he has to provide separate living accommodation for each of his wives and must divide his time equally among them. If he cannot maintain justice in the treatment of his wives, the Qur'an stipulates that he is to have no more than one wife but somehow this is often forgotten. Perhaps we as a religion need to focus on responsibilities more and rights less."

"You are right. Some of our men, perhaps me included, have heard only what they wish to hear."

Ayesha joins the conversation. "Sheik Ishmael I believe I came to you when my husband was married again by you. I knew nothing about this. You were immensely sympathetic but unable to help me at the time. I was desperate and felt that your concerns were with not being alone with me, a woman, rather than hearing the desperation of my position."

"Ah I remember your husband lied to us. He said you knew about the marriage and had consented to its going ahead."

"That is correct, and I want you to know that this led to me attempting to kill myself. Why did you not check with me before he married again? Why was I totally excluded? May I suggest that you speak with the first wife of any man who wishes to marry another. I know of several others who found themselves in the same position as me."

Ali quietly talks over Ayesha. "Please, the sheik is a man of God and deserves more respect. I think the imams need to address the issues you raise but we must all respect each other. If not we will get nowhere."

The imam speaks again but he is now more circumspect. "Ayesha, I know this has been very difficult for you over many years. But I would like you to know that it has also been a complex and difficult issue for me."

"I can assure you it is immensely more difficult for the first wife, and I respectfully suggest that this is your responsibility as our imam and a man of God."

" . . . You are right we need to work together to bring about change."

"Again thank you for speaking with us about this issue that is so often kept away from public discussion, but I am adamant in suggesting that this is your responsibility. No imam should marry a man who has another wife or wives without checking firstly that they are not afraid of violence from their husband and secondly that they agree to this marriage."

After another silence Nalendi intervenes. "Sorry to cut you short. This has again been an enlightening conversation and one that has just begun and we are well over time and the news waits for no man. If you as a listener want to have more input into this conversation please take it back to your community. And of course keep us in the loop as Ali and Ayesha are vitally interested and will continue working on this issue."

"Now before we go a reminder that this is part of our series *No future without forgiveness* and again I am sure that to forgive and forget is not the answer. Clearly with family violence it is essential that all parties remember the damaging cycle that drives the violence. So how does one do this without being overwhelmed by anger and regret? Perhaps we need a particular program to look specifically at how to forgive the perpetrator without forgetting the action. I ask you all to think on this. We look forward to your company again and thank you for your interest. Now over to you John for the news."

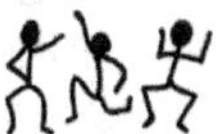

Over lunch Themba says he wants a few minutes with Nalendi.

"This has been a very difficult session to manage. There were so many calls, particularly from irate Muslim men. One threatened to go to our board and another said he would burn our building down if we interfered any more. With him I read

153

back his number and told him I would call the police. Should I do that?"

"And then there was an endless stream of crying women. I was not very good with them. I knew you would not be able to deal with too many of that type of call, so I only let the one through. Now I am feeling that I let them down. This is getting quite tricky. What I did with the women was to speak quietly and refer them on to that lady who called in from the refuge. But can we please have more of a briefing session before the next program because I feel like I'm flying by the seat of my pants."

"And doing really well, but if you are truly feeling out of your depth it may be possible for you to do a short course in dealing with difficult calls. Or you could try Lifeline training. I did it and it was great. But Themba, you did really well. You are actually getting quite superb at your job. You are doing well with both selecting the calls to put through and when, and also at containing those you turn away. Well done. Fantastic work. You are fast becoming my hero."

"It's the manly bit I find most difficult. Woman sort of put it on and invite rescuing." Nalendi leans close, "Like this sweet thing?" She brushes my lips and before I know it we are kissing passionately.

"Oh shit I'm sorry." I turn swiftly and head for the toilet. I must get myself under control. What the hell am I thinking about?

I now head for the phone room and look up Mathue's number. "Hi Mathue I'm in a bit of trouble and I think you might be able to help."

"Sure, can we chat now or would you like to come to my place for dinner. We could go somewhere quiet and chat after that and you could spend the night because I know you live on the other side of town. If you can get to Fish Hoek station I could pick you up there at six and drop you off in the morning to get us both to work on time. Or am I over reacting?"

"No man I need a steady hand as quickly as possible."

"OK, six it is then at the station."

Nalendi comes in and sits on the corner of my desk. "What was that Themba? How about chatting about it after work?"

I look at her and blush. Thank God I called Mathue. "Sorry I can't. I am out to dinner tonight."

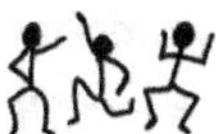

Mathue and I park outside his home and walk up the drive, through an entrance and directly up the stairs to the second floor. As we pass the entrance he reminds me that he shares this house with his parents, his brother's family and his aunt and grandmother. "We all live under the same roof but in quite separate areas. Some people find this strange but we enjoy it. When we meet as a full family it's usually in the pool area and we braai. Everyone loves a good old cook up around the pool, especially the kids."

As we come up the stairs Sarah is there to greet us. "Hi guys, I'll get the kids and we can eat right away because I know you need time to talk."

I'm introduced to Jan and Anna, seven and nine, and they chat away as we eat. The family is relaxed and full of fun. It is great to be part of such a settled family meal. To my surprise I begin to let go of the lump in my throat and am almost sad when Mathue says thanks to Sarah and we head off into a separate living space for some privacy.

"Thanks Mathue, I need help but now it's difficult to start. What I realise is that what I'm about to talk about has been building for a while and I think I wanted to talk to you in particular because of what you have said about taking a risk and going to a place that is uncomfortable because God called you to do so." I laugh nervously "Well I wish I was so noble but I'm not. Out of place yes, out of my depth and about to make a big mistake is my issue."

"Hey slow down. What on earth are you talking about? Have you done something at work? What is it? Take your time we'll work through it."

"Well that's the problem. I'm not sure I want to work it out but I do know its wrong and will complicate my life like hell. But stopping things here is also going to be hard man."

"Themba you're talking in circles and even I can see that you are agitated. Have you spoken out of turn, had a fight with someone, what man, or is it the obvious thing that we could all see coming? Nalendi?"

Now I am sure that Mathue can see me blushing even under my dark skin. I'm going hot and cold and I'm even excited by just thinking about that kiss. I hope to hell I don't go hard. That would be just too embarrassing.

"OK man, clearly its Nalendi. So what do you want me to say? It was bound to happen. It was already playing out at Monkey Bay, only you're too nice to notice. That lady with her swan neck and long eyelashes is too gorgeous for anyone to avoid, especially when you're away from your wife and kids for so long. But I'm speaking too much aren't I."

"Ya man a bit. I can't keep up. Are you saying I was coming on to her before."

"No Themba, I'm just saying that it was inevitable that something would brew. So speak man and I'll try to shut up and listen."

"Well I love Nomalisa and I miss her like hell and I… Oh hell man, that is no excuse. Every time I close my eyes I see Nalendi and today she was teasing me and I kissed her man."

"And?"

"And then I ran away to the toilet and phoned you."

Mathue burst out laughing. "Sounds like you don't need me. Your conscience is working just fine. I'm proud of you. You stopped before you started and now you've told me I'll help. If you're tempted I'm your AA man. Just call before you act.

When did you last call your wife? Sounds like you need to contact her now and tell her you miss her."

Mathue comes over and hugs Themba. "Good man for reacting so swiftly. Overcoming temptation is hard my friend. Maybe we need to support you more. I guess life is lonely over your side of town. Come over this weekend and spend some time with my family? Maybe we can go to the beach and church on Sunday. I can introduce to the mob I'm finding so hard to befriend myself. What do you say man?"

"I say you're talking a lot, maybe because I've embarrassed you. Sorry I needed to get it out and under control. Maybe I'll sleep tonight and thanks I'll phone Nomalisa before I go to sleep and I'd love to visit again on weekend and come to church but you know I'm not sure about the God stuff."

We go back to his living room for coffee with Sarah before I go to phone Nomalisa and bed. That night I dream I make love to Nalendi but don't say a word aloud. To myself I say "get your wife here quick man before you mess up."

Racism or Xenophobia?

Before Nalendi goes on air, she and Themba have an in depth discussion. Both convinced of fireworks on this program, they want to ensure they don't add to political tensions that already exist. They agree that if callers get antsy Themba will suggest calling them back or invite them to text in rather than have them wait while listening.

Themba will also clarify who is a refugee and who South African so that callers can be carefully filtered and the program balanced.

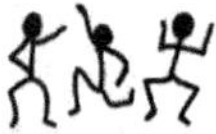

"Hi listeners and welcome to *NFWF*. Today we tackle one of the most difficult issues in our series and I want to begin by quoting Ranjeni Munusamy's 'Somewhere over the rainbow, racism and xenophobia's dark cloud.' I have kept this article in my scrapbook since January:

We have again resorted to the lowest form of human behaviour. Incidents of racism and xenophobia have exposed South Africa as a superficial, ugly, violent nation that lacks respect for other human beings. We are what we are: a nation in decline and at war with itself.

What rendered South Africa's reconciliation project a farce? This was the 'Rainbow People of God', according to Tutu, and we were so thrilled by our unique process of reconciliation that we even exported it to other conflict zones in the world. And now it is coming apart at the seams.

There is a 'low level civil war' in our society, discernible through various forms of violence including racial and xenophobic. 'We have through the lack of self-respect grown to disrespect others. The value of life has diminished. Our sense of identity has been fractured to such an extent that we go out and commit these acts.'

So what can be done? Incidents of racism are dealt with through the courts and institutions like the Human Rights Commission. The police deal with incidents of violence, including xenophobia. But how does this nation heal and learn to stop turning on itself?

We need strong leadership, but not only political. Intellectuals, religious and social formations need to intervene. There should be a fundamental respect for human life and property, without discrimination.

The underlying issues are complex. Unemployment, poverty and crime should never be blamed on foreigners who are themselves victims of the same problems of competing for limited resources in the context of increasingly unregulated trading.

The manifestation of racism and xenophobia is symptomatic of the general decline of our society. Disrespect for others is evident from the top down, from the lack of accountability to hatred of those different from ourselves. For as long as this is not changed and our values are diminished, our society will remain deeply troubled. And history is doomed to repeat itself.

"OK we have a couple of participants here today to talk with you about your issues of racism or xenophobia.

"Sarah and Mathue am I right that you are both working hard at building towards a multicultural community by becoming members of a church where you still feel alien?"

"Yes. But let me start with some history. Sarah and I met in the coloured church and were immediately drawn to each other. We had so much in common. We both loved Jesus and wanted to serve him and it was in our church that we flourished and fell in love. Our lives were centred on our beliefs and much of our time was spent within the church community. Here we lived, laughed and gave ourselves to God. We were happy. We loved each other, our children, our extended family, our community and our spiritual home. We depended on our God. We served in our church and worked towards helping the lost in our community find life and hope. We believed this was exactly where we needed to be.

And then one day while sitting in church I heard God speaking as clear as day. 'Mathue, I want you to visit another church.' I wasn't able to for the next week because of commitments within my own congregation but then the call was so strong that we listened and went. We went once, then twice then almost every second week. I was reluctant and this church felt strange but I wanted to do what God asked of me. And then as we sat in this strange and different service, God spoke again to me. 'It is here I want you and your family to worship regularly and to serve.'

This was hard to hear and almost incomprehensible. Why should we leave the safety of our own coloured people to serve God in this new place? We missed our church so. Why would He want us to move?"

"Thanks Mathue Now we are backed up with calls."

"Great I would love to find out how people deal with racism and xenophobia and maybe we can help each other with how to face these issues."

"Apparently people began phoning as soon as they heard about todays topic so sorry if you have had to wait and let's get to you without further delay. Mum I believe that is what you would like us to call you. You are on."

"Good morning and thank you for taking my call. I am not doing well. I have heard you speak Mathue but what you have been through is nothing.

"I don't want to give my name because I face persecution every day not just feeling bad like you guys. I am scared for me and for my family, for our lives. I've been in South Africa for nine years now. I left my country to save my life because of war, not just people saying bad things, and now we are not safe. Every day we face danger. A neighbour has been killed just because he came from Zimbabwe.

"First there was Xenophobia in 2008 and I was scared and now it is happening again.

"Xenophobia is about the jealousy from our brothers in South Africa. They say we take their jobs and opportunities. But we just make small businesses to get money to live. The way I see it. To make the business takes sacrifice. They don't understand that. It started in KwaZulu from the Zulus. I have family and can't allow anyone to come to kill them. I would rather die. I bought a panga, and have been waiting in my house to see if they come. The Zulu king is not the politician he is a Zulu and wants to be known, so he says bad things about us and now the people have lost lives because of that and the government does nothing.

"I want the people to know I cannot go home to Zimbabwe because I will be killed and now here you want to kill me. What must I do?" M cries and mutters something that can't be heard. Then before either Mathue or Sarah can answer she hangs up.

"I'm sorry M."

There is silence for a while and then Nalendi takes another.

"Mohamed from Cape Town University. I was going to talk about a specific issue but having heard the last caller I will respond to her instead. We are one of the world's most diverse societies and we struggle because of this. Different communities are often deeply intolerant of each other.

"To explain. Apartheid left not only a deep legacy of white-against-black racism. By forcefully ghettoising ethnic groups according to the shades of their skin, colour or because of language and religious difference we now live with a legacy of colour prejudice and of interracial hostility. Add to this the huge migration from the North since 1994, and we have another layer of prejudice against Africans from outside the country.

"As a result, both black and white South Africans and every shade between are deeply suspicious of Africans from north of the Limpopo. But there is another thing I want to throw into the mix. African immigrants are violently attacked because perpetrators believe the police will not prosecute them when the victims are foreign and not 'like us'."

"Thank you sir and I am sorry sister that you are scared. I hope our program will help you. Next caller please."

"I'm feeling bad, my sister. That problem hurts my life. Here in Cape Town, I didn't see anything, but I have family there in Durban and a friend in Joburg. My friend phoned me, he said they were cutting this one lady, and she's dead now. Only God knows, but for us, we don't know what will happen. I don't like South Africa, but I'm staying here because my kids have to go to school. I want to leave because there is no peace here. Now in the Congo, there are a lot of foreigners but nobody does anything to them. President Zuma never liked us, he never liked the people from outside."

The next caller Federico is laughing as he speaks "I am from South America, olive skinned and speak with a heavy foreign accent as you can hear, and yet no one has ever behaved in anything other than a friendly manner towards me. Am I not a foreigner?"

"Interesting, Federico but I think a conversation for another day as there are so many callers waiting. We will just take one more and then respond to these."

"I am so scared as a white woman in South Africa. I am often accosted with wolf whistles, salacious looks and improper remarks from strangers, usually black or coloured men who are playing power games with me." Marie's voice trembles and her uneven breathing on the other end of the phone make her fear palpable.

"I'm scared to be alone at home because there are often break-ins in our area and the crime statistics on the Cape Peninsular are high. I am afraid of leaving home on my own and constantly afraid for my children's safety. So how do I think about xenophobia and racism? It paralyses me . . . and when there are reports of violence of any kind in the community all

I can think about is getting away from this country to somewhere that I can breathe again. God help me!"

"Hi Marie, it's Sarah. I'm so sorry that you are trapped by fear. I know there is always news of violence on the radio and TV and I also know there are break-ins and muggings and hijacks but I've never before really thought what it's like from your side of the fence and I am so sorry it's there. Sorry but I can't help wanting to defend myself by saying that it's not always black on white violence. We live in a suburb which is mainly white and a white guy who lives three houses from us is a drug dealer and we are careful to avoid him and keep our kids away just to be on the safe side.

"But more importantly, I want you to know that there are people like me who want to build relationships without thinking about colour. I think that is why God has called us to a 'white' church and it's certainly why we are part of this project. Please keep listening and maybe you will find a way in to hope."

This call is followed by a silence and then a cutting deep voice demands attention. "Hi Onke here, I am a student at Stellenbosch university and I am fed up with always being asked to look after our scared 'white' sisters. They've had their run. Wasn't that what Apartheid was about? Protecting beautiful selfish white women who did nothing and expected everything. Anyway, on to what I've actually called about.

"Have you heard of 'Open Stellenbosch'? Well our movement is considering the prospect of discouraging foreign students from coming to the university because of widespread racism. For the past three months we've been appealing to the university to address our issues but now because we feel unheard by the university's hierarchy we have decided to draw broader attention to our plight by putting together a YouTube called 'Luister' and we ask you to have a look.

"Just today I heard Mmusi Maimane say the legacy of racial segregation is still with us, the so-called born-free generation, with black students facing greater challenges in getting a tertiary education because of inadequate funds and the poor primary and secondary education system.

If we do get to university, we struggle with basic living expenses and textbooks from which to learn. This limits our freedom to access the opportunities supposedly available to all our people. Until this is changed we won't achieve Mandela's dream of 'building peace, prosperity, non-sexism, non-racialism and democracy.' So until this happens I have no sympathy for Marie's fear."

"OK Onke you are right about black disadvantage and especially for the 30% black youth who are unemployed in our province. Do you have any idea how to change this?"

"Oh Mmusi Maimane gave us a clear answer to that. We can choose either to see the worst in our fellow South Africans and allow our anger and frustration to grow, or we can give power to the ideal of unity in diversity. Which I guess means acknowledging things like Marie's fear. But for me right now it means access to the internet so I can finish my studies."

"Ah well, then it might interest you that someone in NFWF is working on a project to extend cheap internet into all communities."

"Sounds good, but perhaps too late for me anyway. I love your program it's great that you're looking for input from everyone. Thanks, I better go and hit the library. We still get free access there."

"Hi it's Mathue again. I love what you've been saying Onke. We often get caught in a cycle of blame. So I'm going to take what you have begun and try to build on these facts. A large number of people in our country have been dispossessed. Some are South Africans and many are fellow Africans who have fled poverty and tyranny in northern lands from Zimbabwe to Somalia and Nigeria. Then there are the privileged, both black and white, who may be well off because they have worked hard, or because of an unjust history, or perhaps they have used or abused our present system of government. This just is. Where we go from now will determine our future, so how do we give 'power to diversity' like Maimane suggests. He does seem to have some great economic suggestions but can we contribute to these ideas? For me it has meant changing churches so that I can get to know other South Africans. There must be many other ideas."

"We have a caller here who has an 'out there' suggestion. Lets hear it. Hi Ben, talk please."

"Well I am often saddened that we are so caught up in the issues that we don't look for solutions. I was wondering about micro-financing. Is this a way we can support young people who are struggling to live while they get themselves educated?"

Now Themba calls through to Nalendi to say that a surge of messages have flooded the board. The gist of their content: "In South Africa using microcredit to support current spending has been a disastrous and irreversible pathway into chronic poverty."

Mathue intervenes "This is exactly what I meant by blame. Perhaps microcredit has not worked in building small businesses among the poor but can we adapt the model to fit educational needs in bursaries perhaps? Let's not close down ideas without thought."

Now Brian joins the conversation. "I think we also need to allow ourselves to go back to looking at displacement and the restitution for people who were evicted from their homes. While this issue is not addressed, xenophobia and racism, which are almost synonymous, will fester. 'Building peace, prosperity, non-sexism, non-racialism and democracy' like Mandela suggested will not happen while people have not dealt with their past."

"OK, so that leads me onto our next topic in the *NFWF* series." Nalendi brings the program to a close. "On Tuesday next week we will look at the issue of removals under Apartheid. I sometime feel we are going round in circles but while we are talking openly I believe we are contributing to building our democracy. Remember as long as we continue to practice racism and xenophobia we diminish and undermine our society, which will in turn remain deeply troubled; and history is doomed to repeat itself. So sorry to cut you short as we always do but until next time keep thinking and contributing."

"That was much easier than I expected. Mathue is a good mediator. He managed people's differences well. What was it like on the phones Themba?"

"Much easier than expected. Was it OK that I interrupted from the phones?"

"Sure it was helpful."

"Well for me our preplanning worked well too. People were pleased to be phoned back rather than hanging on for ages and the texting in is catching on well. As you saw, lots of messages came in that way.

A weekend in Fish Hoek

I've finally got my sea legs. It's almost like rock hopping. All about balance. By moving forward, head up, torso towards the shore, arms outstretched and using an occasional backward step to steady myself I balanced for a moment, stand on the board and then fall. I gulp, swallow salt water, surface and crawl onto the board again, then off and on again. "You're doing really well uncle" I hear from close by as Ben shoots past with ease and a giant grin.

And then I'm up again and the wind whips past as I finally stand and ride my board. What exhilaration! I rush a hundred meters to the shore, then turn, sit and paddle out again. The wind chills my cheeks, the sun shines but without the ferocious heat of summer. Light glances across the water, and the cloud streaked sky brings the heavens and ocean together in a smudged horizon. This day is gentle. The waves run ahead of the board, then crest and spill a lacy foam which washes up towards the beach then slows, splashes and creeps quietly back to sea. I love the ocean. I love exerting my body and I love being alive.

After an hour of paddling out and surfing in to paddle out again, I am spent. I shiver under my borrowed wetsuit, wipe water from my eyes and stride up the beach, board under my arm. I am at one with the soft sighing ocean, the whispering wind and the shrieking gulls. My skin is taught and tingling, I taste sea water, smell seaweed and am sticky with salt. Now finally I have experienced the generosity of the sea on a day of welcome.

"Maybe next time the sea will be more of a challenge, uncle Themba, but you were really good to get up on the board first go." I smile "Well it was great for me. I'm not a confident swimmer so a quiet introduction is exactly what I needed."

Daniel strides up. "So Themba, you want to walk along the coast to St James and we'll pick you up there? Ben will lead the way. I'll pack the car and follow in a few minutes."

I nod and follow Ben, who rushes off towards a concrete causeway between rail line and rocks and then skips along ahead of me. "Come on, uncle, lets beat them to the station." I increase my pace hoping to share Ben's exuberance but then stop awestruck, my senses flooded. This peninsular is truly magnificent.

I look south. The ridges fade one into another towards the distant Cape of Storms. To my right a precipitous rise of solid sandstone mansions stretch up the hillside to fire charred slopes beneath silver grey sky and to my left a gently simmering sea washes up over rocks and onto the path. Oh, how I would love to live this close to the sea. How spectacular and life affirming it is to be this close to nature in all its power and gentleness. I am so aware that today, a winter's day, is crisp but not cold, The wind is alive but not biting and South Africa is for me the most magnificent, vital and inviting home. It is so far from the turmoil that fills my work life that I can almost forget our crippling politic.

Daniel is waiting at St James station. Ben and I jump in and we drive to Mathue's place where we meet with the extended Kindo family, Marie and Daniel's other two boys, braai fish bought at Kalk Bay harbour and relax for the afternoon.

Our discussion about the internet, connectivity and helping as many Masiphumelele residents as possible get connected is punctuated by calls to catch a ball or settle a squabble about cricket scores. I am hoping to join Daniel on one of his basic training sessions in Masi about using the internet as an online library for high school students. Ben, at nine, is almost as familiar with the net as his dad and also wants to be part of this team.

Mathue is more circumspect. He is a little intimidated by online study but is enthusiastic about garnering support from young people at the church. I of course am very keen to publicise the work once it has some traction.

We all spend the evening making music with the Kindo clan and I fall asleep exhausted after a totally engaging day. This is exactly what community should be about, working playing and dreaming together. I sleep soundly and am wakened just in time for breakfast, and join Mathue in walking to church. His family has gone ahead as I have slept in.

We slip quietly into our seats just as the singing begins. Verse after verse of praise. I'm not sure about the words, but love the harmonies and am soon completely consumed by the mingling of my voice with others in joyful praise. Oh how I love communion. I have been exhilarated and alive with my work, but lonely, and now I am at one with those around me and completely at peace. It is good to be here among friends. The singing joins us into one body, expectant and malleable. Is this what it's about?

First there is a testimony. One of the ministers had left his comfortable coloured community and married a white woman. Together with their three young children they now welcome any person from any country or creed to share in their bounty, never turning any soul away. They thrive and grow by sharing their lives with all God's children. Verses about the Good Samaritan are read from the bible. The sermon that follows exhorts us to watch and pray. Watch out for each other, rich or poor, black or white, citizen or refugee. We are all God's children. All deserve a place. Each is made in God's image.

After the sermon we mingle over coffee before Daniel drives me in to Fish Hoek where I go up to Steers and relax looking out across the railway line toward the sea. I enjoy a rib and chips before heading back to the city and then home for the night.

I wander down to the station ready to wait a while because it's a Sunday but there is a train within five minutes. I hang back as first a teenage girl and then a bunch of young fellas climb on board. I follow, walk past an old couple, sit by the window and contemplate tomorrow. I would love to phone Nomalisa and hear her and the twins babble over each other but decide not to. I don't want another phone stolen.

Suddenly my reverie is shattered by a shrill scream. I look up to see the girl who boarded ahead of me shoved up against the window, a knife at her face. I jump to my feet without thinking and hurl myself between her and her assailant. I hit out and a head bangs against mine. Now I am thrashing wildly. There are arms and legs and constantly banging fists hitting again and again against my head, my torso, my body. They are coming from all sides. A hundred hurtling, hurting blows. Blood, a gurgling sound and then nothing.

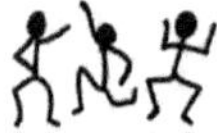

There's a buzz of whispered words, nothing, then more distinct voices. I move my head but stop as a million silver stars sparkle, before a knife of light ends in a explosion of pain.

"He's coming around. Hi Themba it's Mathue. Are you finally with us it's been days?"

I try to open my eyes, to move my head, to focus. I can't, but I can feel the steady pressure of a hand on mine and hear the steady punctuation of a beeping bell. "Ah look his eyelids are fluttering and he's pushing back against my hand. I think he is with us. Come on man we want you back." I listen and try to smile but without much success, and gurgle in an attempt at speaking. Pointless, as there is something blocking my mouth and down my throat. I press again at the hand and then drift away. It is so hard to focus.

What seems like an age later I listen as two voices fill the space above me. "Do you think he will recover soon doctor. His family are on tenterhooks and our listeners at CTT call continually. The flowers keep arriving at work as they clearly do here and people are beginning to need his recovery as a sign of hope."

"Its Nalendi, you said? Yes. He was conscious when he came in but we put him in a coma to help reduce the swelling of his brain. His eyes will take time, so for a while he won't see. The cuts on his face and torso are healing well. He is a strong young man but after such a severe beating it could be a while yet. One knife wound nicked his heart but other than that his internal organs are fine which is a tremendous relief. He will be very stiff and sore for a long time but we will bring him out of the coma soon. In fact give him a couple of weeks and he will be sporting his scars for all to see.

"The police report that the six young tsotsis responsible have been arrested, and the young girl who Themba rushed in to protect is doing well. She has had extensive debriefing, as have the elderly couple who watched on in horror as your young man took the beating.

"Everyone involved will recover from this incident. For me, the sadness lies in the inevitable hangover of fear that such acts generate within our community. How we will rebuild trust when there are so many indiscriminate acts of violence is my concern. Since Themba's admission the papers are again filled with stories of bashings, robbery and rape; perhaps because he has a profile, muggings are as ubiquitous as ever. Well not quite, but almost as if public perception somehow seeds more violence and fear."

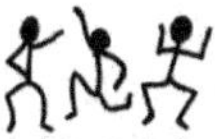

There is lots you can see with your eyes shut. Did you know that you can see different shades of light and the direction that it comes from, a shadow as something comes between you and the light, its direction and its depth. You can also hear the stillness of night, the clicks and buzzes of hospital equipment both close by and at a distance, birds, whispered voices, the clatter of a meal trolley and even the sound of another breathing. It is amazing how alert you become to the world around you.

Because I have had days of focusing on nothing but recovery and experiencing my present I have become super aware of those around me. Some people poke and prod asking about my pain. Nalendi sits by my side and explains what happened to me, the girl, the assailants, and the old couple. She speaks about people's responses to my situation. Their anger, fear and pain. "You know, Themba its like you've become our proxy. People are waiting for your response to this assault. It's not yours anymore its ours and people are waiting for you to take a message to the world for *NFWF*."

Nomalisa also speaks into my darkness. I know she isn't in the room with me although her voice is clean, close and clear. "I love you Themba, but the doctor assures me you are doing fine. He promises that you will speak to me soon. Be strong my hero." Daniel's voice is steady and encouraging, Mathue says little but holds my hand and sits solid and strong, my anchor, and Soda's edgy presence brings life's restless energy into my quiet. Never before have I felt so cared for.

Alone with my thoughts for nights and days without sight, I visit and then revisit my history in an attempt to ground myself and put what has happened into perspective. I am at war with myself.

The muggers were evil. They hurt the girl and then you for no reason. They must be punished. But then why was I not punished when I stole?

Ah because you weren't caught!

Should I be punished now?

No you stole to eat. There was no work. Many stole to eat.

Then my conscience spoke again.

What you did was wrong. You knew this. Remember the encounter with that old lady when you ran. You ran because you knew in your heart that what you did was wrong. What was done to you is wrong so think about justice. They need to be punished.

But what is justice after Apartheid? Well that's easy. When the ANC won power we were promised a new life free from the shackles of white rule, but were given nothing but the vote. We were a new and emerging people with many hurdles to overcome. The black population was poor and marginalised while the moneyed and educated whites were leaving our troubled country in droves. There was no redistribution of wealth, no apology from our oppressors and no political readjustment in our favour. We had to take what we needed to live. This is justice.

Ah so you are owed because you are black and a victim? Because you suffered? Who didn't suffer then? Did your muggers suffer? Did they need a punching bag to let off steam? Don't be ridiculous.

Well as a kid I watched many avoid any consequence for their bad behaviour. People were encouraged by the Truth and Reconciliation Commission to expose their heinous criminal acts and were rewarded by being granted amnesty. Night after night I saw people admitting to torture, murder, and rape, and their victims wailing in agony and perhaps relief at finally knowing the truth of what had happened to loved ones. But people were seldom punished. For them, forgiveness came without punishment or restitution. So I guess my philosophy was 'take what you need, and if that's wrong seek forgiveness later because you are a victim of Apartheid'.

Ah so you are one of South Africa's victims. Why? Because your parents had sad lives, you couldn't access good enough schooling, usurpers came into your country to steal your legitimate place as a jobseeker. There were many reasons. Nothing was ever your fault. Is that what you believe?

Well yes . . . um no. Anyway I'm no longer a teenager and I am now taking my destiny into my own hands and attempting to change my beliefs.

So do you need to take responsibility for past misdemeanours? And another question. Do you need to find a way to rebuild relationships with people you have robbed?

Well after the Monkey Bay weekend I know that talking honestly to others about my life helped me recognise my pain and some of my misbehaviours, take a step towards grieving their loss and letting them go. I could not have done this on my own so in the jargon I read later 'It is in the transaction between people that forgiveness and restoration of relationship happens.'

So thats it?

No. It's also about me finding my own path to freedom. I can't do this for anyone else.

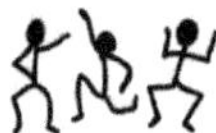

Now that I understand where I am and why, I use the intimacy of silence to think seriously not only about what has happened but also to find some meaning in it.

Because I am working on *NFWF* I have become the embodiment of fear and can use my experience to live out forgiveness. I know personally what it is like to take on the cloak of the outlaw. I remember the alienation, inadequacy and driving anger that led to my crime spree and I know the redemptive energy of looking my behaviour in the face and choosing to turn away.

Once recovered, I will work with my muggers at facing their actions. I will help them hear what it was like for me, the young girl and the old couple to face their violence. Hopefully they will acknowledge their actions, say a genuine sorry and turn from their ways, so that together we can find a suitable atonement.

Thinking about this in forced solitude I come face to face with myself for the first time. I have never thought of either saying sorry or repaying my debt to those I robbed. Perhaps I can find some redemption in using this experience to repay my debt to society. This decision gives me a restless energy and I can't wait to recover.

By the time I open my eyes again and talk I feel like a different man. I have a living mission. I will embody forgiveness.

But now comes the crunch. Without the continual drip of painkillers every movement becomes painful. Stretching out my arm for my glass of water or rolling over and using a bottle to pee in is excruciating. The indignity of needing help for every action is exhausting.

Apology - The Sowetan

Dear Sir/Madam,

My name is Themba and I hope that my apology will be printed in the Saturday edition of your newspaper as this publication has the largest readership.

I write from my hospital bed where I am recovering from a mugging on a Cape Town train. This incident has brought a clarity to my mind that was not here before. When one commits a crime, however small, against another, that person is harmed because you shake their trust in humanity.

In my late teenage years I searched for work but could not find any so for three years I joined a Sowetan gang who stole from people on the streets and robbed homes in and around Soweto in order to support myself.

Now I wish to apologise unequivocally for what I did.

I cannot today restore relationships with those I harmed by stealing from them because they were many and I have long forgotten what I took and from whom. But what I can do is say who I am, apologise openly to the people of Soweto, and begin to give back to society. I hope to do this by working with those who violate me or others, to help them see what they have done and to repair relationships with those they have harmed.

Please help me find forgiveness by accepting this apology.

Thank you

Themba Mkotle.

District Six

"Good morning listeners! Thank you all for your stupendous goodwill towards Themba. He is now awake and slowly beginning to look around and speak with people. Thanks to his NFWF buddies he is seldom alone and he has expressed his gratitude to you all for your continued support. He said yesterday that he feels like the whole of the Cape is supporting him. I will continue conveying your messages so keep on ringing in although I must say we are stretched fielding all your calls without Themba here to help. Now back to our program.

"Today I will start with the story of District Six because it is an iconic reminder of the horrors and legacy of our Apartheid history. The District Six Museum encapsulates one of many Apartheid removals and offers a way of honouring the people affected by such cruel policies. It also generates ways of working with this history to reconstruct community. I will first read a summary to remind you all of what happened in District Six and we will then open the lines to generate a discussion about how we can work at honouring the history of our diverse population and generate a new hope for our future.

"I begin by quoting from Linda Fortune's book The House in Tyne Street. Childhood Memories of District Six. Page 122/123

Our first encounter with a bulldozer was terrifying. Suddenly one morning this big monstrosity rumbles and roars down Tyne Street and comes to an abrupt halt in Chapel Street. Most of the neighbours and their children were running behind it, while other grown-ups had gathered outside their homes to see what the noise was all about. It looked as if a space ship had just landed, as if it had come to invade District Six. 'Can you people now see what's happening here? I told you the world is coming to an end!' one old lady shouted. 'No!' a man shouted back from across the street. 'The world is not coming to an end, we here in District Six are coming to an end!'

"And now to the history for those who do not know it.

Named in 1867 as the Sixth Municipal District of Cape Town was a lively community made up of former slaves, artisans, merchants and other immigrants, as well as many Malay people brought to South Africa by the Dutch East India Company during its administration of the Cape Colony.

After World War II, District Six was relatively cosmopolitan. Situated within sight of the docks, it was made up largely of coloured residents, which included Muslims, called Cape Malays. There were also a number of black Xhosa residents and a smaller numbers of Afrikaners, other whites, and Indians.

Government officials gave four primary reasons for the removals. According to Apartheid interracial interaction bred conflict, necessitating the separation of the races.

They deemed District Six a slum, fit only for clearance, not rehabilitation because it was 'crime-ridden and dangerous, a vice den, full of immoral activities like gambling, drinking, and prostitution.' Most residents believed that the government sought the land because of its proximity to the city centre, Table Mountain, and the harbour.

On 11 February 1966, the government declared District Six a whites-only area under the Group Areas Act, with removals starting in 1968. By 1982, more than 60,000 people had been relocated to the sandy, bleak, Cape Flats township complex some 25 kilometres away.

The old houses were bulldozed. The only buildings left standing were places of worship.

Since the fall of Apartheid in 1994, the South African government has recognised the claims of former residents to the area, and pledged to support rebuilding.

The District Six Museum was established in December 1994 and works with the memories of the District Six experience and with forced removals more generally.

"Our first call is from Jem who was at Monkey Bay with us and I will ask him to talk about the lasting impact of the removals on his community."

"Hi this is Jem and yes some of us ended up being OK but not all of us. Me, my mother and sister were not only moved to the flats but we were also separated from our aunts and cousins, friends and community. The brutal Apartheid system deliberately weakened all of us by separating us one from another. This of course was only part of the cruel plan.

"We now lived on a bare wasteland with nothing around us, and miles from any work. Mum had to travel by train for an hour and a half to work. She would leave at dawn and return after dark leaving us to fend for ourselves while she slaved to put food on our table. She worked while we were in District Six but there we were cared for by aunties. And the so-called criminal element looked after us if we wandered the streets because they knew us and our mums.

"The results of the ruthless act of taking us from our homes and dumping us in the middle of nowhere still impacts us today. I'm OK. I went to university and found work, but Jamma will tell you a little more about those who didn't make it."

"Hi, I'm Jamma, and a huge part of my family still stay in the struggle area; the Manenberg's and the Noble Park's and they didn't make it. They are struggling. Their life is a grind. Unfortunately there is a cycle to this kind of existence.

"If you go to the sub-economic areas the Manenberg's and the Nobel Park's the first thing you must realise is that it is purely about survival. When I go down this road where we used to live and I turn left into this area I actually don't know what is going to happen.

"Three weeks ago I went to my aunt there and a guy stopped his car in front of me on the speed hump and he pulled out a gun. He knew this other chap and it must have been something that had happened before. This chap gave him something and left and I'm just behind him and we were all scared. Although I grew up here you don't know what is going to happen next . . . He could have taken my car or he could as easily have killed me.

"So in Manenberg it is about survival. Now you have this drug problem. We had a gang problem. Where did they get their role models? At first as little boys they walk around with plastic guns. Then they go to school and they see people with money and for them to finish school is not important. They go there and cause chaos. The parent is at work and don't know what's going on unless they are an addict also. So now you have this cycle. How do you get them out of it? Eventually they become addicts and you know what the Tik does to you, to your brain. It becomes a cycle. They move from Tik to becoming a gangster and then they die. This is the Apartheid legacy . . . This is our story."

Nalendi joins the conversation. "Again we are flooded with calls. So if you don't get through I apologise in advance."

"Hi, this is Pieter and I want to say that I think recognition of you as a person is important, someone has to see you as a person before they take care of you. Unfortunately that is not happening for black or coloured people. I think what keeps them ignorant is that the communities are so riddled with these problems and can't get to beyond basic survival. You know Maslow's hierarchy. So at the moment there is no hope. Something needs to be done. It is very hard to get rid of a drug problem without resources. We have got the army, we have the police but the people who run this government need to be concerned about it. It is an issue for them to deal with.

"The drug addicts go to hell. They will flog themselves until they die and the families who are not weak, they have to learn to cope. They survive. I was studying with a nice man whose son was a drug addict and he explained to me how he deals with his son. He was together you know. His life was OK but he was dealing with the issues, which takes another kind of resilience. You learn to go on. You are not OK but you function OK. It is a luxury to break down because your life is becoming crazy with drugs. You have to survive. You have to keep it together just to keep going man.”

“Ja Pieter I agree. Some people have survived despite the removals, but others are still overwhelmed with problems. Places like Manenberg are war zones. I guess the question we face today is how do we, the common people, get our government to take notice. Also what can we as the community do to build hope for our future.”

The next caller takes the discussion back to the District Six Museum. “Ronja here. I am a Swedish exchange student doing research on fishermen around the Cape Province. I’ve come to the museum for a historic overview of the removals. I can’t believe what the government did, but what worries me more is that attitudes under the new government have not changed in the least. Coloured fishermen are still treated with absolute disdain by both black and white.

“There is no fairness in this country. Poverty is staggering, corruption in the fishing communities I am studying is enormous, with quotas ruining the fishermen and making boat owners rich, and the bigotry is as bad as ever. In Langebaan for instance, the old Afrikaner population still keep anyone but their own out of their cafes and shops and treat people no differently to the way they did under Apartheid. The coloured fisherman are asked to leave if they sit at the tables and eat a meal. What has changed? Nothing!”

“I have another caller on line, a tourist this time, from Australia. She says she has something she wants to read about District Six Museum. Go ahead please Ruby.”

I felt physically ill after just a couple of hours with the exhibits, the photographs, the words, the experiences and trauma of so many people. There was much more to see and read. I wanted to understand all of the material available but I couldn’t manage any more and left just to settle myself.

I couldn’t comprehend the numbers, 60,000 people removed from a beautiful inner city suburb, on the slopes of Table Mountain, and forced to live so far away in a wasteland. So far away from everything, family, friends, services and infrastructure, the destruction of a rich and vibrant community with generations of history and connections. Having driven past Khayelitsha the day before made the contrast enormously intense for me.

The exhibit that gave me a sense of the magnitude of the forced removals was the street signs of all the roads that were demolished, hundreds of road names, each representing so many people that would have lived on each street. I was shocked. How could any government believe it had the authority to take such action against its own people, instead of upholding the law to protect its citizens? How could the Apartheid government have taken steps to destroy the lives and souls of one group of its people, while still maintaining it was a democracy?

I felt ashamed by my ignorance of the injustice suffered by so many people in Cape Town. I thought I understood Apartheid in South Africa, I am well educated and have watched the news over many years. Had supported the banning of competition with the South African Rugby and cricket teams, symbolic perhaps, but a possible action for Australia to stand against such dreadful injustice from within a "democratic" nation.

My time in District 6 Museum was profound and affected my emotions for many days. My deep sadness and anger stayed with me. It left me wondering how can "civilised" nations tolerate such overt injustice, just stand by the side and do nothing. It reminded me of the Holocaust, Rwanda and Bosnia, where people watched and did not voice opposition, or take effective action.

How can we humans allow such injustice to happen? The potential for Man's inhumanity to Man shocks me, it is hard to comprehend . . . and when this is perpetrated by a government responsible for protection and refuge? I guess it's no surprise that the process of repair, restitution, and recovery from such trauma still has a long way to go for District Six. It may take

"Thank you Ruby. We in South Africa are so used to these stories that we forget their immense inhumanity. Now thank you to Linda, someone who knows the work of the District Six Museum intimately. Again and again people who have survived the tragedy of being forcibly removed from their homes have spoken about how difficult it can be to truly deal with the trauma of losing a sense of place and community. Linda has led many education training sessions on exactly this topic and we have invited her to talk about the work she does on memory boxes."

"Yes I am very happy to talk on this. As part of my work as education officer at the museum I conducted many tours into District Six, and in doing so I began to pick up little artefacts. A button here, a bead there, and I found enormous pleasure in finding these little pieces, mementoes of my past. So now I began collecting in a more deliberate manner.

"To these collections I would add old precious photos and small keepsakes my family or I had collected. Then at home I would spend time sorting through these, finding exactly the right place for each. For instance I placed small play things that reminded me of my childhood like a marble, an old spinning top and a couple of charms into a special toys box. And so I pieced together remnants of my past life on Thyme Street. This process took time with me spending many long moments simply touching, sorting and creating a space in an old box or tin or other container. Sometimes I would painstakingly create a small replica of a room or a space in which I lovingly placed my precious remnants. In this quiet contemplative process I found a new healing.

"As I worked on my memories I found that each sense led me back to my past, the smell of certain spices, the touch and feel of certain fabrics and so I began to extend my collections to include items that were not old in themselves but nevertheless led me on a journey into memory. These small simple prompts offered me new pathways into old memories and evoked experiences I had lost. With this process came a peace and joy.

"Because I found this so therapeutic for myself I began to run workshops with others, leading them on journeys of remembrance and rebuilding of their sense of place and belonging. This grew and became my work with memory boxes."

"Linda, I love what you have done to turn tragedy and trauma into new beginnings and ask you, listeners, how you might use your own experiences to explore and foster new beginnings. I honestly believe that changing the fate of our country can only happen through healing and I have a suspicion this needs to happen one person at a time. Again we are running late for the news so listeners please think about what Linda has been telling us. Next time on air we will explore what you, the listener, are doing to heal yourself so that you can join the ranks of those who live in hope for our magnificent land and its future."

Welcome back Themba

Utterly alone, I sit cross-legged on a flat rock next to a quiet quicksilver stream. A mild zephyr tickles through my hair. I am neither hot nor cold and after weeks of pain I am finally comfortable in my skin. The view to the horizon is of gently folded velvet hills stretching out to distant mountains.

An old man comes and sits beside me. He smiles and turns to face the sun. "I've come to tell you how important it is to be your own man Themba. Stand strong my son, remember your history and choose wisely." I turn to speak but am awakened by my alarm.

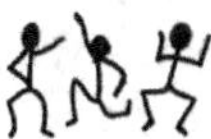

Nalendi picks me up from my room at Elsie's River and drives me in to work. She and the doctor have decided that I need to transition back slowly. As I open my door she leans across and kisses me. "I've missed you Themba."

"And I you Nalendi, but I am a married man and wish to work at bringing my family to Cape Town as soon as possible. So while I am immensely attracted to you I would appreciate you keeping our relationship friendly and professional."

The tears that flow down Nalendi's cheeks shine in the sun. "I respect you and your request Themba shall we go."

"Good morning all. Themba here and it is wonderful to be back. Thank you all so much for your constant support. It's kept me hoping in the darkest places. Now there's much to catch up on so call in please."

Nalendi jumps in "Callers have been waiting from before the news and the board is full. So if you can't get through immediately keep trying. Simon, go ahead please."

"Welcome back Themba you are our hero. Now if there is anything you would like to know about your health just ask. We've been updated daily. Even through the time that you were in a coma so any questions?" . . . Themba's response is a deep grumbly laugh. "No well then what I'm on tenterhooks about is how come you wrote that letter in the Sowetan. Sounds like you've been through the dark night of the soul my man."

"OK, so straight into it then" Themba chuckles. "Well, when I first came to my senses in hospital all I wanted was to ensure my assailants were punished. I wanted them to feel pain like I had. But once I heard they'd been caught and were in remand awaiting trial I started worrying about them. They were all young, and once young people are jailed they are thrown in with hardened criminals. I also thought about my own teenage years. While I had not personally mugged anyone I had almost done so once and without thinking. That stopped me in my tracks."

"Keep going I'm impatient man!"

"Well, Simon, I had plenty of time to consider what made me different from those who attacked me so I began with looking at myself.

As a young man I didn't think about why I stole except that people owed me. This was reinforced by the rhetoric I heard. I was a kid when the ANC won power and we were promised 'a new life free from the shackles of white rule' but what we got was nothing but the vote. We blacks were poor and marginalised while the well moneyed whites left our country in droves. There was no redistribution of wealth, no apology from our oppressors and no political readjustment in our favour.

I also remembered watching the TRC on telly night after night when I was in Saxonwold and confined to my mother's room. People were encouraged by the Truth and Reconciliation Commission to expose criminal behaviour and were rewarded by being granted amnesty. No one faced any consequence.

Night after night I saw people admitting to beatings, murder, rape and the families of victims would wail in agony and perhaps relief at finally knowing the truth of what had happened to loved ones but no one was punished.

At the time I didn't think about my response to this. But as I lay in hospital thinking over and over what the TRC stood for, I realise that watching the broadcasts had taught me that forgiveness came without restitution. So when I stole as a teenager I assumed I would get away with it. It was simply my right to get what I needed and if it turned out that I was wrong I could seek forgiveness later."

"Well if it's like that for you, what about for your abusers? Should they just get away with it?"

"I have thought a lot about this, Simon and I realise that as victim I see things differently. My muggers must be held responsible but I'm not sure traditional justice will help them change. My understanding of the criminal justice system is that the offender has a passive role. He faces trial, then conviction and finally punishment. Sometimes incarceration helps the criminal change but more often he learns new tricks from the old hands he meets. He often leaves prison armed for a more effective criminal life. This is particularly the case with young offenders I believe."

"OK so?"

"I want my muggers to know they caused considerable damage and pain and I also want them to understand why it's important for them to stop offending. If they have to face me, the young girl they attacked and the old couple who watched they will see and hear from us the effects of their behaviour. Hopefully this will help them understand their destructiveness and give them an opportunity to say sorry. Because they were violent I think this will have to happen alongside the normal justice processes. But it's my hope that by getting to understand what they did to us our muggers will want to find some way they can redress their actions and restore their relationships, with us in particular and society in general."

"Wow that's novel."

"Apparently not, Simon. Restorative Justice is often used and particularly with young people. Mr Google says RJ works because it not only helps repair the harm caused by offending but also restores relationships by providing an opportunity for active participation by victims, offenders and their communities."

Nalendi joins the conversation "Well Simon, does that answer your question?"

"Extremely well thanks."

"OK, any other questions about RJ before we go to more general calls?"

"Hi. Piet here and I'm sceptical. Is there any evidence that this works?"

"Yes, Piet, there is research that offenders who have been through RJ are less likely to commit further offences than similar offenders who are subject to more conventional interventions. There is also data that indicates that RJ is empowering for the victims."

"Thanks for waiting Rachael go ahead."

"I'm pleased you are recovered, Themba and welcome back and I'm sorry to argue with you on your first day but I am sick of this go easy on offenders hogwash. If you really want to show remorse, hand yourself in to the police in Soweto. There are so many of us who have been violated in one way or another and I think it is about time that we as a society gave a strong message. If we don't make people responsible for their actions, violence will just continue escalating. You are right that the TRC did nothing so we must act now to stop violence and corruption. I want to live safely and it's the government job to make this happen."

"Not sure where to go with that one, Rachael except that I respect Themba's right to think about a different way. Perhaps we can look at government responsibility at another time."

"Hi I don't want to give my name. It's so good to know you are recovered enough to be back and thinking so clearly Themba. We were all so scared for you. South Africa is scary and you can never tell where danger will come from next", a small voice whispers. "What happened to you took me straight back to a time when I was raped and there was no one there to rescue me. I've never got over it. The police didn't find my attacker and . . ." the caller gulps back tears "I've been scared for the last five years. I can't go out alone and I've got fat so that no one will want to touch me again . . ." and then the line drops out.

"Oh wow! I'm sorry." Themba says.

"How dare people dump on you like this on your first day back Themba. South Africa is scary but there are some of us civilised enough to let you settle back before we burden you with our stuff."

"It's Paul isn't it? I'm fine and I think it's important to look our issues in the face."

"I certainly agree with that Themba, but because we follow your exploits on the radio you have become family to many of us so your life has become ours. I for one find myself wanting to either protect you, punish those who hurt you or admonish you when you don't do things by my rules. So forgive me for jumping in to defend you although that is exactly what got you in to trouble on the train, man. I think we should stand together as a civil society and look after each other.

"With your letter, I want to yell at you 'Don't admit to any weakness. Look after your interests. Protect yourself and let the muggers pay their dues'. But on the other hand we need to find a way to give everyone a stake in our society and then maybe people will behave better. If that happens perhaps we can feel safer and begin to take down the electric fences and talk to each other. So at the end of my rambling, thanks Themba, you do us proud. Keep up the good work and look after yourself buddy."

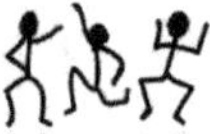

Themba gets a call from Nomalisa. "Greetings my love. Good program and as always I'm proud of you. Now are you sitting, because I have some sad news? Your Umkhulu has died. Your mum and Sizani are on their way home and you will want to go also I am sure. It will eat into our savings but you must go, so we will come to Cape Town later."

"How, when, what happened?"

"He was old Themba that is all, and now he has gone. Go well with your people my love."

Within hours I am on a plane to Pietermaritzburg, then in a bus to Impedle.

I am greeted by Noxolo and Sizani and then immediately whisked off to help slaughter an ox as a gift to our ancestors. In our tradition burial is seen as a celebration of transition from one stage of life to the next and our observance of the correct rituals is important. We burn impepho to communicate with our ancestors and drink utshwala together to celebrate our life as a community because they ensure our ancestors continued interest and guidance. For me the beliefs associated with the Zulu tradition have waned, but I loved and respected my grandfather. He gave much time to guiding and shaping me and I want very much to honour his leaving. Also, if I'm honest, there is still a little bit of me that is scared that he may come back and bring trouble to me or my family if I don't follow his rules.

I sit with one arm around Noxolo and the other around Sizani. We watch as the setting sun filters red gold light through waving grass then drops sudden as a stone and Venus winks her way into the night then welcomes stars from tarnished horizon to the end of our fading vision. It has been so long since we last sat together as family. I have forgotten my love of their sunlight smell, the crispness of Noxolo's dress against my skin, the softness of Sizani's dark honey skin against my own. My heart thumps heavy and hard against my chest. I

190

pick up its rhythm and sing a lullaby from my childhood. Sizani sings clear and high in harmony and Noxolo hums quietly. We are at peace.

Noxolo is now old and tired but overflows with stories about my wonderful babies who consume many of her waking moment. "Two together is too much. If one is good the other is mischievous and because they have each other they do not worry about our language. They dance and sing and keep us busy with feeding and playing and loving. You are a lucky man, Themba, Nomalisa is a wonderful mother and cares for me well. You must bring her to you soon my son. It is not good for her to live alone."

Sizani lives with a man and has a baby daughter but has not yet married. She is beautiful and full of life and I am sad that I do not have more time to be with her. This reunion is wonderful, all consuming and too short. As the night air cools, we say good night. My ladies retreat to Gogo's hut and I go off to join my impi brothers.

For them the night is young and they have many stories to share. I sit and watch the sparks from the fire swirl up towards the star filled firmament. This too I have missed. And yet in truth I sat here seldom as a man and then only by initiation and not yet fully grown. But I watched often from the dark beyond the fire circle and listened to the bragging talk of virile young men, each carving out his place as one of many and yet unique. Now finally it was my turn to sit among my peers and speak my life into my clan and nation. But alas this was not to be.

"You are not our brother you are a coconut, a throw away to the New South Africa. You are a traitor. You have gone against our code by talking about what happens inside yourself to the outside world. No Zulu warrior speaks as openly as you do of his feelings and none admit their nefarious exploits. You are an outsider no better than those who come like cockroaches from the north. We will not deny you in front of your mother because we are proud Zulu men but know that you are not one of us and therefore not welcome in Impedle. This is no longer your home and we are not your brothers."

I reach into my pocket and rub my stone for comfort. Now every part of me aches. I am an exile.

Back to Monkey Bay

This time I rattle down to Monkey Bay with Soda. He has specially borrowed a beat up van for this jaunt and is very excited that he is my guide. We open our windows wide and invite the intemperate elements to blow through the cabin, which leaks anyway. The sun shines, the sky is azure and only the smallest scattering of clouds intensifies the brittle beauty of spring.

We have left Bo-Kaap early because Soda wants me to see the surroundings in which the secret Grailstone can be found. He takes me to the end of a road and points to the west. "We cannot go there, only scientists may enter, but my heritage has been uncovered in the earth around that stone. This is my sacred site and I want you to know about it. You come from the great Drakensburg Mountains, well my heartbeat began here in the womb of my mother's grandmother's before I was born."

As we sit together and drink our Coke suspended eighty meters above the rocks looking out across the Atlantic Ocean I understand that Soda's integrity is built on the knowledge that his people have roamed this land for many generations. He, like me, longs for the acceptance that comes from belonging to a land, a tribe a nation. We are born of Africa, and Africa will always be our home.

I have not seen Soda sit still for so long before but now he jumps up, bows and turns a circle before laughing at me "Come on man we have to get on with the show and who knows how long it will take to get to Monkey Bay in this old bomb."

We are almost the last to arrive.

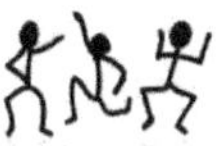

It is wonderful to be here again and I quiver, senses flooded. The buzz of conversation is intense but held by its counterpoint, a gentle background thunder of ocean, a whisper of insects and the wind sighing through the fynbos. The air heavy with humidity, and warmth brings closer the platinum sky smudged against the translucent ocean. The smell of salt, sun-touched bush and sea lure me out and away. But the hammer of my heart, rush of blood through my body and tightening in my throat remind me that I am here to dream, collaborate and invigorate our cause, Ubuntu.

Informal greetings done, Nalendi stands to begin. "It is a pleasure to be here again six months after our first encounter, although for most of us there have been many meetings between then and now. It is my task to remind you why we began our journey together and to prepare you all for the work of this time together. Our initial task as a group began in response to a rise of xenophobic attacks across the country. We were to be part of an experiment that might help to build, in a small way, towards a better, more inclusive future for South Africa.

"Lamentably our country seems to spin from one disaster to another even worse. You will all have read Yusuf Abramjee's letter and I will draw from this as preparation for our continued work together.

"He says to Mr Zuma:

I implore you to imagine being an ordinary citizen without the benefit of a security detail and every measure protecting me from threats at my home, my workplace, on the street, in public spaces and in my car. Imagine living in fear all the time. This is the environment that millions of citizens are living in. You have to be blind to reality if you miss the desperation of citizens and the equal helplessness of law enforcement.

You said that an attack on our police is an attack on the state. Mr President, your assessment is correct, but talk is empty. What is being done? Many members of the public have lost faith in the police and the criminal justice system.

Widespread corruption, poor leadership and bad service delivery has eaten away at the respect that these institutions should be able to demand.

The lives of our citizens count for even less it seems. Some 47 South Africans are murdered on average every day and once again your citizens have to take responsibility for a problem that the state should be tackling with all means at its disposal.

The rot is so widespread, the stink overwhelming. Desperate times need desperate solutions. Listen to your people who are the terrorised and persecuted.

"Abramjee then uses the Marikana disaster as an example of how over and over again people take the route of escalation rather than looking for the path of peace and reconciliation.

"He prescribes a well-known model for the way forward. Show the way, inspire a shared vision, challenge the process, holding leaders responsible for their actions, enable others to act and encourage the heart by rewarding those who achieve the shared vision.

"So here we have a path that is tried and true. I wish Zuma would listen.

"But until then let's turn again to our task, remembering firstly that South Africans are wounded by their violent past, while foreigners are wounded by wars and poverty in their countries of origin, and secondly that untreated trauma is the cause of xenophobic attacks in this country.

"Our task together is difficult and limited, but worthwhile as we contribute to the healing of our country, which is an imperative."

Nalendi stands silent for almost a minute and then says "Simon, over to you."

"It's a pleasure to welcome you all back. Our task over the next day is simple. Today, go in to your original groups, track your achievements and create a symbolic presentation to bring back to the main group. Tomorrow we will share our presentations and celebrate together as *NFWF*."

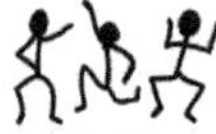

Alison leads the way to our group room but is soon overtaken by a dancing Soda.

"It's so good to see you all, but no chatting. Grab a piece of butcher's paper and a felt pen and draw a timeline of the last six months, naming any instance where your life has been touched by, or you have contributed to, the work of *NFWF*. When this is done write a short title which encapsulates your highlights."

I'm into it immediately. Wow, I've achieved so much. Getting *NFWF* happening, facing my own excruciating past, talking about myself on CTT, learning how to listen to others, taking part in the mountain search, keeping in touch with all participants, staying in Daniel's house, being mugged, almost having an affair, talking to my conscience, writing a letter of apology, talking about forgiveness and restitution on radio, facing my grandfathers death, my alienation from my Zulu brothers, and now back here to face the outcomes of my journey.

I sit looking at each peak and trough along my line. Tears well up and flow as I remember my humiliation at being the 'token' black. I feel the sharp knife through my clenched jaw as my detractors revel in my distress.

As I trace my timeline I allow myself to enter again my deepest experience of each memory. When the pain is intense I take out my stone and rub it. Feel its smooth surface between finger and thumb, weighing its mass. I ground myself and move on. As I enjoy the highs I look around and try to make eye contact with one of these wonderful people who now mean so much to me. When I catch someone's eye I hold the deep warmth that begins with a flush of my cheeks and then moves through my body. I love the virile surge as I know my manhood. These people have helped me become a secure spirited man.

So what will capture this extraordinary journey? How do I put words to my new belief? I see a corrupt government, a South Africa in dire circumstances, poverty, lack of infrastructure and escalating violence but I now have positive hope that each South African can and wants to grasp a new vision for peace and prosperity. What image captures this? Community, strength, humanity? All sound too static, without passion, overused English. Come on Themba you are a journalist. Find the words. I can't. And then I remember my mother tongue. There is a much used, perhaps overused word but it captures my wish for my country, ubuntu. Now the title for my timeline is clear. Ubuntu is built one soul at a time.

I look around and realise that my friends have been quietly waiting for me to finish.

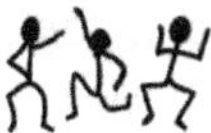

We now each read the title we have given our timeline and consider how these can be brought together. Soda begins, "My life's lekker man. Because of *NFWF* I got my first job in years. The museum's now got me dancing around leading tours through my beautiful Bo-Kaap because of you Themba, so every day I'm introducing visitors to my wonderful world and talking about how we must remake history. My title is Sharing history builds community."

Linda follows saying "My life is full.

"I'm writing a new book and leading history tours but am still thrilled by every opportunity *NFWF* gives me to talk about the Apartheid removals, trauma, memory boxes and healing. I believe it's healing that is most important. My title is Sorting memory heals trauma."

Warren follows "I have continued to live life as completely as possible. My mentorships of disadvantaged students are important, as is my work through my church. My timeline title is Recognise the image of God in every man."

Ricardo says his title is similar to Warren's but comes from trying to see the good in those who behave badly towards him. "There are often those who mistreat me because I am poor and look different but I now take special care to let them know that I can help them move towards freedom through my forgiveness. My title is Love your enemy as yourself."

We smile as we all recognise that in the last six months each has contributed to building a stronger and more potent civic identity. Now how will we create one punchy title and find our symbol. Our title comes easily. Ubuntu is built by listening, loving, healing trauma and forgiving, one soul at a time.

Finding a symbol is more difficult but finally we decide that each shape a small figure from clay. The individual figure can have a head bowed, cocked listening, talking, or looking up, but all must have outstretched arms. When each person has shaped their figure I join them together because I am most familiar with clay. I mould the arms of each body around the next to form a close-knit circle, make a clay base and scratch our title out on the clay. We have our symbol of ubuntu. Our work is done.

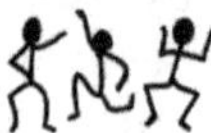

An afternoon tea gulped down, all thirty of us head for the beach.

Here we run into the breeze, laugh and celebrate being together. As we race towards Kommetjie we play a word game. What should we name our walk? Just then a bound of baying dogs joins our pack followed by flurry of flustered owners. We hurtle headlong into the evening and collapse together effervescent and overflowing with words and life.

As the afternoon cools with the sun behind Chapman's Peak, we all meet in the main conference area, each small group sitting together. Nalendi welcomes us all as beloved comrades. We laugh, and a couple of the guys jump up and to attention. Simon smiles at us and begins. "We will now pull together our presentation to the sponsors. We'll begin by each group presenting their symbols to us all, and then finding a way to bring them together. Who will go first?"

We present and discuss our symbol of ubuntu. Then Albert stands and begins to talk about their TIK symbol with a no entry sign.

But it's as if there is no energy in the room. We go through the process of listening to each group, but the mood is depressed, almost lifeless. People fidget. Albert excuses himself and goes out for a smoke but doesn't even bother to move to a place we can't see him.

Finally Simon stops us and asks, "OK what is going on? No one is showing any interest in what we are doing."

"It's like we are just recycling all the old South African problems, and worst of all we aren't even mentioning Xenophobia which is the reason that got us together in the first place. How are we going to be able to solve these problems if all the great minds in universities and even experts from outside of South Africa have no ideas? South Africa is just fucked. It's heading for annihilation and there is nothing our small crew can do. However nice we are."

"Come on people it's not that bad is it?"

"Yes it is. Every time you turn on the radio or TV something else has broken down. Electricity, sanitation, housing, violence, homelessness, corruption, when is it ever going to end and the damn ANC and Zuma do nothing but find ways to add to their personal wealth. They are taking 'their turn to eat' to an extreme and now the police are being killed so we can't even depend on them. Why should we damn well hope? It's hopeless."

Now there is silence but everyone is deeply engaged. "There is nothing we can do, let's face it."

Then Marie and Dianne begin to wail. A groaning wild harmony of anguish and one and another joins in until everyone is wailing, a deep heart wrenching endless lamentation. It is excruciating, intense and savage. Pent up anger and pain pours out of us. It goes on, and on and on. Some people have their arms around each other while others sit alone. But the weeping keeps us each separate in our alienation and fear and together in our desolation. Our hearts are breaking.

And then slowly it stops and first one and then another sits empty and exhausted. Nothing more to give. Grief spent we look at the floor and then walk from the room to sit in fading light. Nothing is said. We are done.

An hour later we reconvene, sitting quietly together in the empty room. I look at each person in turn, recognise my strong ties to each one of these, my soul mates, then lift my head and tentatively begin to sing Nkosi sikelel' iafrika.

Slowly first one and then another voice joins mine until all are singing and then Soda jumps to his feet and dances around the room. Now we stand together and continue singing. Finally Simon says "OK people lets sit down and look at what has happened over the past couple of hours."

We sit and after a while Brian says, "How can we put our anguish into words?"

"It is beyond words, and yet a voice is what *NFWF* offers. A place where people can speak the unspeakable. It has become the mouthpiece for many so we must find them the words, or betray those who have invested their faith in us."

"I'll try. We cry for freedom lost first to Apartheid and again to our protectors, who now strut and plunder instead of lead. We weep for South Africa, ourselves, our land."

"But all is not lost. By being with *NFWF* I have found hope in many small things."

"In Namaqualand" Sienna says "where I come from, the desert dies for winter. There is no blade of grass. It is as if God has abandoned the land and then in spring there is the rain and one small leaf is followed by another until the whole landscape is filled with flowers of red and gold and blue. Every colour of the rainbow shouts 'a new season has begun.'"

"It is true that our country seems beyond saving but there are some small signs of hope. Nalendi, there is that letter you read to us when we arrived from Abramjee. We still have some freedom in our press and Mmusi Maimane seems to be a good man with some ideas for our future."

Nalendi jumps to her feet. "And come on people, we have done some great work. We have done more than just name the problems. Our callers keep telling us that we are making a difference in their lives. At least once a program we are thanked that we voice people's concerns, but also give them a forum for sharing their learnings, sadness and joy. They could not be more effusive. Even the knockers are pleased to have a forum where they can be heard and they clearly articulate that *NFWF* is part of them finding a place to be heard."

Soda jumps up excited again. "Our symbol is important except it was maybe better when it was short like Themba said. *Ubuntu is built one soul at a time.* I think we see it all the time in *NFWF*."

Nalendi responds, "Ayesha, would like to tell us about your 'small' success."

"Oh I would love to. You know how I was working with the chief iman about family violence in the Muslim community. Well, there was this lady I will call Sarai. She phone CTT for help and was directed to me and I visited the chief imam on her behalf.

The imam said he knew the family well and had heard Sarai's story from her husband. He asked me if I was aware that she had done many things against the religion and had caused great hardship for her husband. When I asked him to meet with Sarai he was very reluctant but eventually we arranged a suitable place and I attended the meeting with her.

At first the imam admonished Sarai and told her she had gone completely against her faith by denying her husband's second wife and added that she had caused great hardship by leaving her older son at home with no one to care for him. At this point I stopped him and said 'you listened to her husband why will you not give her the same respect.' I also reminded him that this was exactly the sort of situation we had been talking about in the meetings organised together with his imam's council. He was clearly shocked and angry that I had challenged him but finally agreed to let Sarai speak.

He was immensely distressed to hear that Sarai had not known about the second marriage but even more upset to hear about her injuries. Sarai's husband had broken her arm, three ribs and given her a severe concussion. He had also broken his son's arm when he had stepped in to defend his mother.

After this meeting the imam went back to Sarai's husband to ask about the things she had said and when he met with us again he reported that the husband had been evasive and that this had convinced him that he needed to listen more carefully to both sides in any domestic dispute and promised to raise this gently with his brother imams whenever the issue come up.

Now a month after this meeting the imam has become a great champion of the work we have begun and Ali and I will soon speak together with the refuge worker about what measures need to be put in place to spread the teaching throughout the Islamic Council of Cape Town. Here is one decisive win for us."

"And of course we have our own hero, Themba. We must not forget him."

I smile. "Thanks Daniel, but I think I am but one of many, or perhaps not many but at least a few so perhaps our symbol of Ubuntu is the one to present to the sponsors when we meet with them tomorrow."

Everyone agrees and I, as the shining star of *NFWF*, am designated as our spokesperson. I bow and agree to carry this pleasant responsibility and our work for the evening is complete.

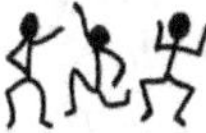

Before bed I sit alone, pen in hand and write my brief for the sponsors tomorrow.

We your NFWF posse would like to take this opportunity to thank you our sponsors for the ride of our lives. It's amazing to look back over the past six months and see the impact of this opportunity on our lives.

Thank you for supporting this brave experiment.

We have all taken NFWF on board so fully that we've become quite wretched that we've not been able to cure South Africa of all its ills.

You know we first told our stories, and then took time to reflect on difficult memories and begin grieving. Next we were invited to start forgiving ourselves and others so that we could let go of what impeded us.

This done, each small group championed a joint issue and shared this with all at Monkey Bay. Of interest is that none of us decided to look at either xenophobia or racism directly but the issue has been raised time and again by NFWF listeners.

From here CTT looked to shape radio programs that would move listeners towards becoming involved in a different approach to engaging with issues, each other, our communities and perhaps, grandiosely, our nation.

Sadly we as a force of twenty five at NFWF have not changed the soul of South Africa. However I would like to chronicle a couple of new beginnings.

We acknowledge that it is through NFWF that hundreds of people are now sharing their stories, facing their pain and looking for their own solutions. Our audiences have told us that we have engaged them in a way that other programming has not and I quote 'It is wonderful to be listened to as an expert on my life rather than as a contributor to already established views on the topic at hand.' We love that audiences are engaging with us and each other as contributors who hope and wish to contribute to a more inclusive future.

Now on to a small number of individual contributions.

Marie has decided to tackle her fears by inviting people from different political backgrounds to begin discussing politics on Facebook. This growing community openly raises political issues and seek solutions together.

Ayesha, Ali and another couple of people are particularly looking at the issues of family violence in Muslim communities and working to change the culture of control within the leadership.

I with help from others am researching the use of restorative justice as an addition or alternative to the traditional justice system, and as you know I am using this process with those who mugged me recently.

Some are becoming involved in volunteering when emergency services need support.

There are many other examples of us raising awareness and supporting positive action within community. Having said this, it is hard not to be overwhelmed by the huge difficulties South Africa has in keeping our country safe. But we are proud of our small successes.

In yesterday's reflection on our progress, we began realising that the changes we catalyse come one person at a time. We believe that this of itself is important and we celebrate that through each person we come one step closer to ubuntu. So now on behalf of our Monkey Bay posse I present to you our sponsors this symbol of our success.

Is there a place for the individual life within history

I look up and she smiles. I touch her cheek and her lips with mine, caress her naked breast, reach down her slim body hungry for her response but there is none. She lies inert. Right here but like a stone and out of reach. I look up to see her expression. Her eyes will tell me what is happening. But I can't see her face. Then her body is gone.

She's not here and I'm alone with my aching need of her. Where are you my love? I have almost forgotten your face, your eyes, your touch, your smell, your heart beat next to mine. It has been too long and now even my dreams are empty.

It is when life is full that I miss Nomalisa and the twins the most. I tried to phone her tonight without success. Where is she and why was she not answering? She promised when we last spoke that she would keep her phone with her.

Honestly, I'm not sure that we will make it. Six months is a long time and we just don't have the money yet for her to move down and join me. I have begun looking for a house to rent in the Fish Hoek valley because despite my experience at the station, this is where I would like to bring my family.

Both Mathue and Daniel have said they could help me find some household basics and reckon the church might help as well, but somehow Nomalisa's enthusiasm has faded in the last week or two and I have begun to wonder if she just doesn't want to come. I'd better ignore my promise and fly up to Soweto for a visit. I'm sure I can manage a short compassionate day or two. My marriage is important and I need to find out what's going on. I will ask Nalendi how to go about this when we get back to work, or perhaps once the sponsors meeting is over tomorrow. I will try Nomalisa again in the morning. Perhaps she has taken an extra shift. I get under the covers again and try to sleep.

An early run on the beach with Soda clears my head. The air is crisp and clean and the sky blue. The wind is cold and from the South West. It whips the ocean into a long low swell of small, unbroken waves, which hit the beach with force. There is no spray and with the tide on its way out the beach is washed flat and is firm underfoot. It is too early for dogs or horses and the only other bodies on the beach look like Mathue and Daniel who are running towards us at speed. They must have been up before dawn. Today will be perfect. Energising in the morning while we sit and listen and then warm as the sun reaches its zenith towards midday. The afternoon promises a balmy farewell walk along this blissful shore.

At breakfast the conversation is congenial and effervescent and everyone jumps up as soon as Simon asks us to move through to our working space. We are all confident and excited about meeting our sponsors and the CTT Morning Management Team.

A row of twelve chairs lines a newly raised stage. A spotlight shines above a podium and there are two half circles of chairs facing it. This formality builds suspense.

We come in and uncharacteristically sit in quiet expectation. Within moments the stage is filled with well turned out individuals and we begin.

Nalendi thanks people, and invites our chief sponsor to address us. He begins "It is good to be here. *'No Freedom Without Forgiveness'* is the project we are sponsoring for 2015, and we take great pleasure in joining you today. Simone, could you please come up and take us through our market research to date."

"Certainly Terrance. We have been following the progress of the *NFWF* project since its inception, and I am happy to report that it is doing exceedingly well.

"Now on this slide you can see that there are three ways in which we measure success. Firstly we have logged the number of calls coming in to your program from the day that *NFWF* began until three days ago. This includes calls that were put through to the program as highlighted in green, those that were answered but did not make it onto the program in yellow and those that were not answered in red. When these are tracked against numbers logged using the same methods for the three month leading up to *NFWF* you will see that the number of calls answered during the program have remained more or less stable but the number of calls to reach the station and those not answered have increased threefold. This is a spectacular result.

"On the second slide I have tracked a survey conducted with 100 randomly selected listeners who were asked to comment on how they rated *NFWF* against four other talk back programs on a ten point scale. As you can see here *NFWF* was rated at a 9 where others rated between 4 and 7. When asked to explain their ratings most participants said that what was important was that *NFWF* valued them as people, not just as callers interested in the issues being discussed. Other questions were asked but I do not wish to cloud this presentation with too many facts.

"Finally, on this the third slide I show the number of calls logged to CTT in relation to (a.) *NFWF's* involvement in the mountain rescue and (b.) Themba's mugging and recovery. While these numbers are not compared with a base line they show an extraordinary buy-in from our listening public. Clearly the personal relationship *NFWF* has built with its listener base is huge. This cements this project as the most successful in the past five years of talkback radio. Now back to you Terrance, and thank you for this experience. I, as a new listener to CTT, am thrilled to be part of this team."

Terrance thanks Simone and turns to the audience. "Well done you! And now I believe you, our prized team, have a presentation to the sponsors."

I jump up and join Terrance on the podium, but then I freeze. It was all very well writing my speech but it's another thing presenting to all these bigwigs. I am sweating profusely and can't find a way to begin. In fact I haven't felt so faint since I came out of hospital. I stutter a beginning but am interrupted by our resident clown, Soda. Unhappy with my timidity he has jumped to his feet and is exhorting the others to stand and clap their support for a frightened brother. Of course they all immediately jump to his bidding. The clapping starts slowly but then shifts up a gear into a thunderous refrain. Themba, Themba, Themba. Now Soda summersaults across in front of the stage and bows to me.

I have become so fond of this fellow who has learned through the school of hard knocks how to brazen his way through any situation. I can't help myself, I laugh and invite Soda to come and stand by my side. He jumps up and joins me and my nerves subside. Now my speech comes easily and Soda slips away unnoticed. As I finish talking Soda reappears with our handcrafted symbol and again people start clapping. But this time those on the stage are as involved as the audience. Tears stream down my face as I say thanks to everyone and leave the stage.

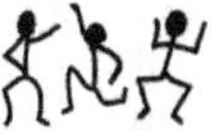

Nalendi takes the mike and introduces the CTT Morning Manager who stands and tells the assembled group how pleased he is with the success of the project. This done he hands the mike back to Nalendi who says she would like to tell us a story.

Once upon a time, there was an old man who used to go to the ocean to do his writing. He had a habit of walking on the beach every morning before he began his work. Early one morning, he was walking along the shore after a big storm had passed and found the vast beach littered with starfish as far as the eye could see, stretching in both directions.

Off in the distance, the old man noticed a small boy approaching. As the boy walked, he paused every so often and as he grew closer, the man could see that he was occasionally bending down to pick up an object and throw it into the sea. The boy came closer still and the man called out, "Good morning! May I ask what it is that you are doing?"

The young boy paused, looked up, and replied "Throwing starfish into the ocean. The tide has washed them up onto the beach and they can't return to the sea by themselves," the youth replied. "When the sun gets high, they will die, unless I throw them back into the water."

The old man replied, "But there must be tens of thousands of starfish on this beach. I'm afraid you won't really be able to make much of a difference."

The boy bent down, picked up yet another starfish and threw it as far as he could into the ocean. Then he turned, smiled and said, "It made a difference to that one!"

I think this boy's philosophy sits well with us.

Now I'd like to tell you how we wish to proceed with *NWFW* in the next six months. The sponsors have decided to support our ongoing work, but with a difference. We will go back to our listeners and invite them to contribute to our content planning by raising issues of interest to them. We will then facilitate discussion as we have done to date and where it becomes obvious that we need professional input we will seek this.

As far as you our Monkey Bay crew are concerned we would invite those who are interested to become our reference group, who will convene when necessary but at least once three months from now and again at the end of our project. Before I hand back to the boss, I want to thank you all for the time of our lives, invite you to relax after this and join us for a special celebration lunch before heading back home.

"Like all bosses I want to have the final say. But before I do so, Themba, can you please join me on the stage." I go and stand beside the podium. "Now I know that one or two of you guys have been helping behind the scenes but I hope what I have to say to you Themba will come as a surprise.

"Firstly you may have noticed that your wife has not been answering your calls lately and that is because she has been very busy with a couple of your mates in Fish Hoek. Nomalisa can you join us up here too please."

Nomalisa walks into the room with two of the most gorgeous little people, who rush ahead and are at my side before I know it. She, my beautiful, composed wife walks slowly towards me with a huge smile. I can't wait and jump off the stage and scoop her into my arms totally unaware of anyone but her. Tears of course before she gently turns my head towards the stage where a sea of smiling faces welcome me back. Hand in had we join them and I bend and then sit on the floor and embrace my beautiful twins.

"When you are ready. No on second thoughts stay there, but listen to me if you can. Themba, we at CTT are impressed with the energy and creativity you have brought to our morning program and as reward we have decided to make you a permanent member of staff and to change your duties. You will now become an assistant announcer and researcher for CTT and as a bonus we have paid for the removal of your family to Cape Town. And with Nomalisa's help, Nalendi, Daniel and Mathue have rented accommodation in Fish Hoek. I believe Mathue took you to see the house and you liked it. And ah, yes, as there is still a little work before you can move in we have booked you into the cottage you are staying in at the moment for another three days. Now I think that is all I have to say except of course another thank you."

Everyone jumps to their feet and thunders into applause while I sit dumbfounded with a sheepish grin on my face. I cannot believe what I have just heard. It is simply to good to be true.

As the applause finally dies down Nalendi comes up on stage, ruffles Suzi's hair and says to Nomalisa. "I believe you can sing. Seeing that Themba is lost to us, could you lead us in our national anthem?"

Nomalisa's honeyed contralto fills the hall and everyone moves into a circle and joins her. What a wonderfully fitting finale. My voice cracks with emotion as I stand with a child on each arm and sing my heart out.

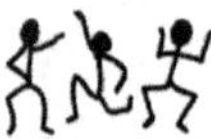

The lunch is long and wonderful and filled with laughter but finally it ends and I take my family past our cottage, where they have already unpacked, down through the fynbos, along the board walk, across the rocks and on to the long sandy beach. Suzi and Little Themba immediately begin digging in the sand as Nomalisa and I stroll a few paces closer to the ocean, sit and look out to sea. "I have dreamed this last long six months of bringing you here my love. Thank you for waiting."

Acknowledgements

Contributors to the history and stories used in this book:

Thank you for the generous sharing of your own histories. Thank you also for being prepared to look at what has changed in South Africa from before the end of Apartheid until today.

Ali, Ashley, David, Doreen, Elaine, Garnet, Jill, Linda, Lloyd, Marcy, Mark, Mike, Nawahl, Nazley, Nula , Patrick, Reza, Ricardo, Rochelle, Ruby-Jo, Samuel, Sean, Tanyan and Warren.

Contributors to background:

Father Michael Lapsley and Dr. John Steward

Research, collecting stories, scribing and editing and immense support and partnering:

David Parris

Glossary

A

AIDS The Aids policies of the former South African president Thabo Mbeki's government were directly responsible for the avoidable deaths of more than a third of a million people in the country, according to research by Harvard university.

South Africa has one of the severest HIV/Aids epidemics in the world. About 5.5 million people, or 18.8% of the adult population, have HIV, according to the UN. In 2005, there were about 900 deaths a day.

But from the late 1990s Mbeki turned his back on the scientific consensus that Aids was caused by a viral infection that could be fought – though not cured – by sophisticated and expensive medical drugs. He came under the influence of a group of maverick scientists known as Aids denialists, most prominent among whom was Peter Duesberg from Berkeley, California.

In 2000, Mbeki called together a round table of experts, including Duesberg and his supporters, but also their opponents, to discuss the cause of Aids. Later that year, at the International Aids conference in Durban, he publicly rejected the accepted scientific wisdom. Aids, he said, was brought about by the collapse of the immune system – but not because of a virus.

The cause, he said, was poverty, bad nourishment and general ill-health. The solution was not expensive western medicine, but the alleviation of poverty in Africa.

ANC. The African National Congress (ANC) is the Republic of South Africa's governing social democratic political party. It has been the ruling party of post-apartheid South Africa on the national level since 1994, including the election of Nelson Mandela as president from 1994-1999.

Apartheid was (in South Africa) a policy or system of segregation or discrimination on grounds of race.

Athlone is a suburb of Cape Town located to the east of the city centre on the Cape Flats, south of the N2 highway.

Athlone Technical College is the oldest Further Education and Training (FET) Institution in South

Africa with a history dating back to the beginning of the 20th century.

Four former technical colleges; Athlone College, Cape College, Sivuyile College and Western Province Technical College were officially merged on 1 February 2002 to become the College of Cape Town.

The College of Cape Town is situated in the central area of the Peninsula, and serves the greater Cape Town area, including a large percentage of traditionally disadvantaged areas and townships. Although the majority of its students hail from the greater Cape Town metropolitan region, the College accept students from all other regions of South Africa, Namibia and other African countries, and many countries abroad.

B

Bergie is a term used for a subsection of homeless people in Cape Town, South Africa. The word originates from the Afrikaans berg meaning "mountain."

Table Mountain National Park runs from Devil's Peak, the Twelve Apostles, and Orange Kloof to Hout Bay in the north-west, the suburbs of Constantia and Tokai before stretching from Cape Point, as far north as Scarborough on the Atlantic coast and Silvermine.

Bobotie is a well-known South African dish consisting of spiced minced meat baked with an egg-based topping.

Bloubergstrand is a suburb of Cape Town along the shores of Table Bay, about 25 km to the north of the city centre of Cape Town.

P W Botha would go on to hold a variety of high-profile positions and by 1966 became the minister of defence, using his position to push for an increasingly militarised country. Upon John Vorster leaving office in 1978, Botha became prime minister. By the '80s, with national and global pressure to end apartheid rising, Botha's regime authorised armed attacks in nearby countries like Botswana and Zambia, where ANC activists had taken refuge and also utilised the State Security Council to kill in-country agitators.

In 1984, Botha was elected to the South African presidency with the creation of a new constitution that would extend some political representation to the Asian and coloured (mixed ethnicity) populations, but grant no power to blacks. Domestic protest grew dramatically and Botha called a national state of emergency in 1985, where, subsequently, thousands of citizens were detained without trial.

Boer, (Dutch: "husbandman," or "farmer"), a South African of Dutch, German, or Huguenot descent, especially one of the early settlers of the Transvaal and the Orange Free State. Today, descendants of the Boers are commonly referred to as Afrikaners.

Boer War. The South African Boer War begins between the British Empire and the Boers of the Transvaal and Orange Free State. The Boers, also known as Afrikaners, were the descendants of the original Dutch settlers of southern Africa.

Boetties (*buties*) means brothers

C

Camps Bay is a bay side suburb close to Cape Town.

The Cape Flats consists of a vast number of townships where the majority of coloured and african people live. As is consistent with the composition of the population, most of the townships are coloured townships and only four are home to africans.

Even with exotic sounding names like Bishop Lavis, Steenberg, Hanover Park, Bonteheuwel, Manenberg, Elsies River, Langa (sun), Nyanga (Moon), Gugulethu (our pride), Khayelitsha (our new home) and many others, living in the townships is not for the faint-hearted. For the most parts, the townships are dreary places, bordering on qualifying for the description of "urban ghettoes". Houses are usually tiny and overcrowded, and in most townships, there are blocks upon blocks of flats which are equally tiny and serve as a breeding ground for gang and other unsavoury activities.

The maintenance of buildings and roads is virtually non-existent, though in all fairness, I need to record the fact that over the last ten years, some attempts have been made to make the townships look more presentable by the painting of houses and blocks of flats, tarring roads and turning big sandy fields into playgrounds. This has, however, mostly been in the coloured townships and african townships continue to look quite appalling.

An interesting phenomenon, which clearly reflects apartheid planning, is that african and coloured townships, in some cases very close to each other, are separated by open strips of land, a highway or the railway line. It is amazing how effective these strips of "no-man's land" were, in keeping african and coloured communities separated.

Fires. On 1 March 2015, fires starting in Muizenberg, spread rapidly across the Cape Town south peninsula.

The **Casspir** is a Mine-Resistant Ambush Protection Vehicle that has been in use in South Africa for over 30 years. It is a four-wheeled, four-wheel drive vehicle, used for transport of troops. It can hold a crew of two, plus 12 additional soldiers and associated equipment. The Casspir was unique in design when launched, providing for passive mine defence. The main armoured steel body of the vehicle is raised high above the ground, so when a mine is detonated, the explosion is less likely to damage the crew compartment and kill the occupants. The cross-section of the hull is V-shaped, directing the force of the explosion outwards, further protecting the occupants. The vehicle also offers crew protection from small arms fire. The capabilities of the Casspir were the basis of the outline capabilities required by the U S Marines for their Mine Resistant Ambush Protected or MRAP vehicle project.

Cetshwayo kaMpande was the last king of an independent Zulu nation. He faced the British in the Anglo-Zulu War of 1879, and was sent in exile to Cape Town when his forces were ultimately defeated. He was restored after appealing to Queen Victoria, but was forced to flee in the face of civil war. His death shortly after may have been the result of poisoning.

Colour and classification. An Office for Race Classification was set up to overview the classification process. Classification into groups was carried out using criteria such as outer appearance, general acceptance and social standing. For example, it defined a "white person" as one who "in appearance is obviously a white person who is generally not accepted as a coloured person; or is generally accepted as a white person and is not in appearance obviously a white person."

Coloured education. The system of racial segregation in South Africa known as apartheid was implemented and enforced by a large number of acts and other laws. This legislation served to institutionalise racial discrimination and the dominance by white people over people of other races. While the bulk of this legislation was enacted after the election of the National Party government in 1948, it was preceded by discriminatory legislation enacted under earlier

British and Afrikaner governments. Apartheid is distinguished from segregation in other countries by the systematic way in which it was formalised in law.

Coloured people is an ethnic label for people of mixed origin who possess ancestry from Europe, Asia and various Khoisan and Bantu ethnic groups of South Africa

Corruption. As the world remembers the passing of global icon Nelson Mandela, the fact that he was a man of principle is a clear element of his success as a leader and overall greatness. He understood the vital importance of the constitutional principles of accountability and the rule of law. He not only said as much, but also demonstrated the courage of his convictions by submitting himself before the courts when summoned to defend his decision to set up a commission to investigate alleged racism, corruption and nepotism in South African rugby.

It is therefore saddening to see how far some in the ruling elite have strayed from the example set by this great man. An important barometer of the extent of this problem is growing public sector corruption, whereby public funds are being diverted away from the public good towards private interests. Private sector corruption is also a problem, but until corruption in government is managed, private sector corruption will continue to flourish.

Crossroads is a high-density township in Cape Town, South Africa. It is situated near Cape Town International Airport and borders Nyanga, Philippi, Heideveld, Gugulethu and Mitchells Plain. Crossroads is one of Cape Town's largest townships.

D

The Democratic Alliance (DA) is a South African political party and the official opposition to the governing African National Congress (ANC). The present leader is Mmusi Maimane who succeeded former Mayor of Cape Town and Premier of the Western Cape Helen Zille on 10 May 2015.

Damelin is a private college, with 17 campuses, owned by Educor group. It was founded by Benjamin Damelin in 1943.

Desmond Tutu, In 1978 Desmond Tutu was appointed general secretary of the South African Council of Churches and became a leading spokesperson for the rights of black South Africans. During the 1980s he played an unrivaled role in drawing national and international attention to the iniquities of apartheid, and in 1984 he won the Nobel Prize for Peace for his efforts.

Archbishop Desmond Tutu was the chairman of South Africa's Truth and Reconciliation Commission (TRC). The TRC was created by Nelson Mandela's Government of National Unity in 1995 to help South Africans come to terms with their extremely troubled past. It was established to investigate the violations that took place between 1960 and 1994, to provide support and reparation to victims and their families, and to compile a full and objective record of the effects of apartheid on South African society.

District Six was an area in Cape Town at the foot of Table Mountain, near to the harbour and the City Bowl. It acted as the gateway to Cape Town. District Six was a cosmopolitan area. Priests, teachers, school children, prostitutes, families, politicians, midwives, gangsters, fishermen, pimps, merchants and artisans lived in the area. They came from all over the world and different corners of South Africa and together created a rich mix of different cultures.

They also introduced in South Africa a strong political tradition. The area was a seedbed of ideas and activities. Most of the people who lived in District Six were working-class. They wanted to live close to the city, harbour and factories where they worked. Rich with memory, it was a place, which has made a great contribution to the history and culture of Cape Town, and indeed to South Africa.

F

False Bay is a body of water defined by Cape Hangklip and the Cape Peninsula in the extreme South-West of South Africa.

Fish Hoek is a coastal town at the eastern end of the Fish Hoek Valley on the False Bay side of the Cape Peninsula in Cape Town, South Africa. Previously a separate municipality, Fish Hoek is now part of the City of Cape Town.

G

Grassy Park is a suburb in the Western Cape Province of South Africa, situated on the Cape Flats in the City of Cape Town.

Green Point is an affluent suburb of Cape Town, South Africa located to the north west of the central business district.

The **Griqua** are a subgroup of South Africa's heterogeneous and multiracial Coloured people, who have a unique origin in the early history of the Cape Colony.

Group Areas Act was the title of three acts of the Parliament of South Africa enacted under the apartheid government of South Africa. The acts assigned racial groups to different residential and business sections in urban areas in a system of urban apartheid.

Gogo. Zulu name for grandmother.

H

Heathfield is on the main line from Cape Town to Simon's Town. Main Road (which runs from Central Cape Town through to Simon's Town) runs along the west of Heathfield.

Healing of Memories workshops offer processes for:
- ♣ facilitating the healing process of individuals and communities in South Africa and internationally
- ♣ remembering the apartheid years and healing the wounds
- ♣ redeeming the past by celebrating that which is life giving and laying to rest that which is destructive
- ♣ working in partnership with others who share our vision

Hottentot first recorded in the 17th century and was a name applied by white Europeans to the KhoiKhoi. It is now regarded as offensive.

Bo-Kaap is the spiritual home of the Cape's Muslim community and is known for its brightly coloured houses and situated at the foot of Signal Hill. Bo-Kaap, one of Cape Town's most colourful suburbs and has a fascinating history. Many of the residents are descendants of slaves from Malaysia, Indonesia and various African countries, who were imported to the Cape of Good Hope by the Dutch during the 16th and 17th centuries.

The slaves were known as "Cape Malays." The Bo-Kaap is also known today as the Cape Malay Quarter.

Helen Zilla. Otta Helene "Helen" Zille is a South African politician. She is the current Premier of the Western Cape, a member of the Western Cape Provincial Parliament, the former leader of South Africa's opposition.

Homelessness and inadequate housing. Since 1994, national government has provided over 2.3 million houses and in the last eight years has developed policies focused on in situ upgrading, improving informal settlements where people have already erected structures for shelter.

However, housing continues to be built on poorly located land far from work opportunities and social facilities. In addition, the upgrading of informal settlements and the provision of low-income rental units has not met demand. There is a growing problem of homelessness and inadequate housing. This huge demand for housing has led to the poor resorting to "illegal" housing options such as the occupation of bad buildings, settlement in informal areas, or homelessness.

Bad buildings are poorly maintained buildings, threaten the health and safety of occupants.

I

Impi is a Zulu word for any armed body of men. However, in English it is often used to refer to a Zulu regiment, which is called an *ibutho* in Zulu. Its beginnings lie far back in historic tribal warfare customs, when groups of armed men called impis battled.

Impedle is a small village in the foothills of Natal's Drakensburg mountains close to the town Howick.

Inkatha. (definition) A tightly woven grass coil is placed on the head to carry and ease the weight of a heavy burden. It is woven in a way to prevent it from crumbling and breaking. Also used as a head protection when fighting. Its symbolism is similar to the *fasces* in Italian culture, that power comes from working closely together and being bound together as one.

Apart from its day to day use, a special *Inkatha* was worn as the Zulu crown. It was kept in a secret hut of the Zulu royal house and it was believed that Zulu kings derived their powers to rule from Inkatha. The British destroyed it when they raided Ulundi and burnt the royal palace during the kingship of Cetshwayo ka Mpande in the 19th century.

Inkatha has great significance in Zulu culture as it represents the spiritual and political powers of Zulu kings and the Zulu nation.

The Inkatha Freedom Party (IFP) is a South African political organisation, established by Chief Gatsha Buthelezi, which encouraged a resurgent Zulu nationalism and created a platform for Buthelezi to advance his political ambitions.

Buthelezi used the name Inkhata which was rooted in a previous Zulu cultural movement called Inkatha Yenkululeko Yesizwe (Inkatha Freedom Nation) which was formed in 1928 by King Solomon Dinizulu.

In 1975, Chief Gatsha Buthelezi formally launched the Inkatha Cultural Liberation Movement to fan Zulu nationalism and pledge allegiance to him. This movement was later constituted as the non racial political party, IFP. The headquarters of the IFP were in Ulundi, the former capital of the apartheid era KwaZulu homeland.

J

Jacob Gedleyihlekisa Zuma, GCB is the President of South Africa, elected by parliament following his party's victory in the 2009 general election. He was reelected in the 2014 election.

Jimmy La Guma was president of the South African Coloured People's Organisation and member of the Central Committee of the South African Communist Party, which was the first nonracial political party in South Africa.

K

Kaffir (Arabic *kafir*, a non believer) – a derogatory term used against black people.

Kalk Bay is a small fishing harbour on the Cape Peninsular. It is also a suburb which has always housed people of diverse colours.

Khoi-San The Khoisan people of the Northern Cape are descended from two different tribes. An amalgam of the original San hunter-gatherers and the later-arriving KhoiKhoi, they were virtually annihilated by subsequent settlers. But the Khoisan culture lives on through some of the most compelling rock art on Earth.

The Khoisan believe strongly in a trickster deity who can be both foolish and wise.

Khoisan is a term used by physical anthropologists to distinguish the aboriginal people of southern Africa from their black African farming neighbours.

The original San hunter-gatherer groups lived on this land for over 100,000 years before the arrival of other black people and European settlers. When the pastoral KhoiKhoi appeared 2,000 years ago, they saw people similar to them in physical appearance, but with a different culture. They called these elders of the land 'the San', which means 'people different from ourselves'.

The San men usually hunted antelope using bows and arrows smeared with poison. Before a hunt, a shaman would conduct a religious ceremony. He would enter a trance and his vision was recorded on a rock by way of painting. This rock art is now a central feature of our heritage.

Kleptocracy is a term applied to a government seen as having a particularly severe and systemic problem with officials or a ruling class (collectively, kleptocrats) taking advantage of corruption to extend their personal wealth and political power. Typically this system involves the embezzlement of state funds at the expense of the wider population, sometimes without even the pretence of honest service.

Kommetjie is a small town near Cape Town about halfway down the west coast of the Cape Peninsula, at the southern end of the long wide beach that runs northwards towards Chapman's Peak and Noordhoek.

The area is a popular for surfing, since powerful waves from the Atlantic Ocean rise up over rocky reefs formed by hard sandstones of the Table Mountain Group. Wherever the bottom is rocky, the shallower waters are thick with giant kelp forests. Kommetjie is famous for its excellent cray fishing.

Khayelitsha is a partially informal township in Western Cape, South Africa, located on the Cape Flats in the City of Cape Town.

Kroeskop. Frizzy hair.

L

Lekker is the Afrikaans word for delicious.

Lobolo or **Lobola** sometimes referred to as "bride wealth"or "bride price" is property in cash or kind, which a prospective husband or head of his family undertakes to give to the head of a prospective wife's family in consideration of a customary marriage.[1] Historically, this property was in cattle, but over time it has moved to being mostly in cash. Some people still practice the tradition of offering cattle, or even a combination of cattle and money. The primary purpose of lobola is to build relations between the respective families as marriage is seen as more than a union between two individuals.

Load shedding is a rolling blackout, also referred to as rotational load shedding or feeder rotation, is an intentionally engineered electrical power shutdown where electricity delivery is stopped for non-overlapping periods of time over different parts of the distribution region. Rolling blackouts are a last-resort measure used by an electric utility company to avoid a total blackout of the power system. They are a type of demand response for a situation where the demand for electricity exceeds the power supply capability of the network. Rolling blackouts may be localised to a specific part of the electricity network or may be more widespread and affect entire countries and continents. Rolling blackouts generally result from two causes: insufficient generation capacity or inadequate transmission infrastructure to deliver sufficient power to the area where it is needed.

Rolling blackouts are a common or even a normal daily event in many developing countries where electricity generation capacity is underfunded or infrastructure is poorly managed. Rolling blackouts in developed countries are rare because demand is accurately forecasted, adequate infrastructure investment is scheduled and networks are well managed; such events are considered an unacceptable failure of planning and can cause significant political damage to responsible governments. In well managed under-capacity systems, blackouts are scheduled in advance and advertised to allow people to work around them, but in most cases they happen without warning, typically whenever the transmission frequency falls below the 'safe' limit. Rolling blackouts are also used as a response strategy to cope with reduced output beyond reserve capacity from power stations taken offline unexpectedly such as through an extreme weather event.

M

Madiba. Nelson Mandela was also known by his clan name Madiba. The term is used as a sign of respect and affection. Why Nelson Mandela is called Madiba Nelson Mandela was also known by his clan name Madiba. The term is used as a sign of respect and affection.

Mandalay is in Mitchell's Plain a township of Cape Town

The Marikana massacre was the single most lethal use of force by South African security forces against civilians since

1960. The shootings have been described as a massacre in the South African media and have been compared to the Sharpeville massacre in 1960 The incident also took place on the 25-year anniversary of a nationwide South African miners' strike.

Controversy emerged after it was discovered that most of the victims were shot in the back and many victims were shot far from police lines. On 18 September, a mediator announced a resolution to the conflict, stating the striking miners had accepted a 22% pay rise, a one-off payment of 2,000 rand and would return to work 20 September.

The strike is considered a seminal event in modern South African history, and was followed by similar strikes at other mines across South Africa, events which collectively made 2012 the most protest-filled year in the country since the end of apartheid

The Marikana massacre started as a wildcat strike at a mine owned by Lonmin in the Marikana area, close to Rustenburg, South Africa in 2012. The event garnered international attention following a series of violent incidents between the South African Police Service, Lonmin security and the leadership of the National Union of Mineworkers (NUM) on the one side and strikers themselves on the other, which resulted in the deaths of 44 people, 41 of whom were striking mineworkers killed by police. Also, during the same incident, at least 78 additional workers were injured. The total number of injuries during the strike remains unknown. In response to the Lonmin strikers, there were a wave of wildcat strikes across the South African mining sector.

The first incidents of violence were reported to have started on 11 August after NUM leaders opened fire on NUM members who were on strike. Initial reports indicated that it was widely believed that two strikers died that day; however, it later turned out that two strikers were seriously wounded, but not killed, in the shooting by NUM members. This violence was followed by the death of another eight strikers, police and security personnel who were killed in the following three days.

Masiphumelele is a township in Cape Town, South Africa, situated between Kommetjie, Capri Village and Noordhoek. Initially known as Site 5, the township was renamed Masiphumelele by its residents, which is a Xhosa word meaning "We will succeed."

Melktert is a traditional Afrikaans milk tart desert.

Mitchells Plain is a largely coloured township about 32 km from the city of Cape Town. It is one of South Africa's largest townships. It is located on the Cape Flats on the False Bay coast between Muizenberg and Khayelitsha.

Modderdam is a small industrial suburb on the Cape Flats.

Monkey Valley. Nestled amongst ancient Milkwood trees and overlooking 8 kilometres of Noordhoek beach is Monkey Valley Resort. World's apart from city living yet only 25 minutes to the centre of Cape Town – Monkey Valley Resort is an atypical splendour tucked onto the southern slopes of Chapman's Peak Drive.

Mossel Bay is a harbour town of about 60,000 people on the Southern Cape. It is an important tourism and farming region about 400 kilometres from Cape Town, and 400 km west of Port Elizabeth, the largest city in the Eastern Cape. The older parts of the town occupy the north-facing side of the Cape St Blaize Peninsula, whilst the newer suburbs straddle the Peninsula and have spread eastwards along the sandy shore of the Bay.

Muizenberg is a beach-side suburb of Cape Town, South Africa. It is situated where the shore of the Cape Peninsula curves round to the east on the False Bay coast.

Mmusi Aloysias Maimane is a South African politician, the leader of South Africa's opposition Democratic Alliance political party since 10 May 2015, and the Leader of the Opposition in the National Assembly of South Africa since 29 May 2014.

My Broertjie My Bra was a song from Kramer and Petersen's 'District Six the musical' which opened in October 2002 at the Baxter Theatre in Cape Town. This musical first exploded onto South Africa's stages in the late eighties and attracted audiences from all walks of life in their hundreds of thousands to the theatre.

N

The Nationalist Party (NP), in full National Party of South Africa, Afrikaans Nasionale Party van Suid-Afrika (1914–39, 1951–98), also called New National Party –(1998–2005), People's Party or Re-united National Party (1939–51), South African political party, founded in 1914, which ruled the country from 1948 to 1994. Its following included most of the Dutch-descended Afrikaners and many English-speaking whites. The National Party was long dedicated to policies of apartheid and white supremacy, but by the early 1990s it had moved toward sharing power with South Africa's black majority.

Nkandla is the private home of South African President Jacob Zuma, situated about 24 km south of the town of Nkandla in KwaZulu-Natal. There has been public controversy about the use of public funds to make improvements to the compound which were said to be for security reasons which cost over R246 million. A report of the Public Protector has found that

Zuma unduly benefited from these improvements. The controversy is sometimes referred to as *Nkandlagate*.

Nkosi Sikelel' iAfrika (*God bless Africa*) is South Africa's national anthem but was also the anthem of resistance under Apartheid.

Noordhoek is situated 30 minutes from Cape Town's city centre in the tranquil farm atmosphere of the Cape Peninsula.

Noxolo is mother of peace a Zulu term of endearment for mother.

O

Ocean View was established in 1968 as a township for coloured people who had been forcibly removed from so called "white areas" such as Simon's Town, Noordhoek, Red Hill and Glencairne by the former apartheid government under the Group Areas Act. It was first called Slangkop and the first resident moved in 1 August 1968. It was ironically named Ocean View, with residents being removed from their previous sea-side homes and views. As a result, its history is embedded in apartheid, and there is still much bitter resentment among many people.

Oudekraal is possibly one of Cape Town's best kept secrets. It is a beautiful boulder-enclosed bay with its very own seal colony, carefully sandwiched between Bakoven and Llandudno.

Set against the backdrop of the Twelve Apostles, with a number of sheltered coves and small sandy beaches between the massive granite boulders, this scenic area forms part of the Table Mountain National Park, is sheltered beneath Milkwood trees and offer fantastic views of mountain and sea.

P

Pen Tech (Cape Peninsula University of Technology), is the only university of Technology in the Cape. and is also the largest university in the province, with over 32,000 students.

Plettenburg Bay. At the end of the 18th century the first Dutch people settled in the Plettenberg Bay area, and in 1778 the Governor of the Cape of Good Hope, Baron Joachim Van Plettenberg visited the Bay and named it after himself. It was around the same time that Robberg (which means mountain of seals) was named because of the large colony of Cape fur seals that resided on the peninsula. In 1910 the first whaling station was set up on Beacon Island and in 1960 Plettenberg Bay became an exclusive holiday town for South Africans.

The PSA (*Public Servants Association of South Africa*) is a registered trade union. The PSA is the largest, politically non-affiliated, fully-representative union in the Public Service, with more than 235 000 public sector employees as members.

Q

Quota man. Most South Africans in the 1990s conceded that it was not enough to simply repeal discriminatory laws, but that remedial action would be needed to overcome the legacy of past discrimination. Hence the Constitution in 1996 was anchored in the concept of non-racialism and equality before the law, with a sub-section authorising the taking of "legislative and other measures designed to protect or advance persons…disadvantaged by unfair discrimination."

The Employment Equity Act allowing the appointment of black people with no proven capacity but "the potential to acquire the ability to do the job."

R

Rastafari is an Abrahamic belief which developed in Jamaica in the 1930s, following the coronation of Haile Selassie I as

Emperor of Ethiopia in 1930. Its adherents worship Haile Selassie I, emperor of Ethiopia (ruled 1930–1974), much in the same way as Jesus in his Second Advent, or as God the Father.

Robert Mangaliso Sobukwe was a South African political dissident, who founded the Pan Africanist Congress in opposition to South Africa under apartheid. In 2004 Sobukwe was voted 42nd in the SABC3's Great South Africans.

Rhodes. Cecil John Rhodes, in full Cecil John Rhodes (born July 5, 1853, Bishop's Stortford, Hertfordshire, England - died March 26, 1902, Muizenberg, Cape Colony [now in South Africa]), financier, statesman, and empire builder of British South Africa. He was prime minister of the Cape Colony (1890–96) and organiser of the giant diamond-mining company De Beers Consolidated Mines, Ltd. (1888).

S

Saxonwold is one of Johannesburg's older exclusive leafy suburbs steeped in the history. Its palatial homes are built on large allotments. Being one of Joburg's most central suburbs Saxonwold is surrounded by places of interest and entertainment value like the Johannesburg Zoo and Gardens and the beautiful Zoo Lake.

Shack fires on new years day left three people dead and 4 000 homeless in Khayelitsha and Thembeni. The blaze destroyed over 800 shacks leaving more than 3 000 people homeless. Three men died in the fire after being engulfed in flames and could not escape.

Shaka was a great Zulu king and conqueror. He lived in an area of south-east Africa between the Drakensberg and the Indian Ocean, a region populated by many independent Nguni chiefdoms. During his brief reign from 1818 to 1828 more than a hundred chiefdoms were brought together in a Zulu kingdom which survived not only the death of its founder but later military defeat and calculated attempts to break it up.

Shebeen.   Illegal or unlicensed drinking venue, In South Africa, shebeens are most often located in townships as an alternative to pubs and bars. Under apartheid indigenous Africans were barred from entering pubs or bars reserved for those of European descent.

Originally shebeens were operated illegally by women who were called *Shebeen Queens* and was itself a revival of the African tradition that assigned the role of alcohol brewing to women.

Simon's Town, sometimes spelled Simonstown, is a town near Cape Town, South Africa, which is home to the South African Navy. It is located on the shores of False Bay, on the eastern side of the Cape Peninsula.

A **skelm** is a crook.

A **skollie** is of South African (Afrikaans) origin and has many meanings: A naughty, dirty or ill-mannered child or a gangster. "Cape Town, busy, crowded tavern of the seas, is plagued by young mulatto hoodlums who work in gangs and are called skollies."

Soweto is an urban settlement or 'township' in South Africa, southwest of Johannesburg; with a population of approximately 1.3 million (2008, Joburg archive).

Soweto was created in the 1930s when the White government started separating Blacks from Whites. Blacks were moved away from Johannesburg, to an area separated from White suburbs by a so-called cordon sanitaire (or sanitary corridor) this was usually a river, a railway track, an industrial area or a highway etc., they did this by using the infamous 'Urban Areas Act' in 1923.

Soweto became the largest Black city in South Africa, but until 1976 its population could have status only as temporary residents, serving as a workforce for Johannesburg. It experienced civil unrest during the apartheid regime. There were serious riots in 1976, sparked by a ruling that Afrikaans be used in African schools here; the riots were violently suppressed, with 176 striking students killed and more than 1,000 injured. Reforms followed, but riots flared up again in 1985 and continued until the first multiracial elections were held in April 1994.

T

Tata means father.

Tamboerskloof is a neighbourhood of Cape Town, South Africa. It lies on the slopes of Lion's Head and Signal Hill, adjacent to the neighbourhoods of Gardens

Tik is a South African nickname for *Ice*, the drug methamphetamine.

Trevor Andrew Manuel is a South African politician who served in the government of South Africa as Minister of Finance from 1996 to 2009, during the presidencies of Nelson Mandela, Thabo Mbeki and subsequently as Minister in the Presidency for the National Planning Commission from 2009 to 2014 under President Jacob Zuma.

Trojans. In Athlone, Cape Town, Western Province (now Western Cape),the area around Alexander Sinton High School became a gathering place for anti-apartheid protests, particularly by students. On 15 October 1985, members of the security forces shot and killed three young people who were part of anti-government demonstrations. On the day of the incident, Security and Railway police worked together to crush a gathering of youth who were protesting against the apartheid government. This incident became known as the *Trojan Horse Massacre*.

A South African Railways truck was loaded with crates close to the edges all around, with the middle unloaded to create space for the police to hide. The truck drove down Thornton Road into the middle of the protest with armed police hidden behind the crates. Then the armed police hiding behind the crates sprang up and opened fire killing three young people.

Truth and Reconciliation Commission (TRC) was a court-like restorative justice[1] body assembled in South Africa after the abolition of apartheid.[2] Witnesses who were identified as victims of gross human rights violations were invited to give statements about their experiences, and some were selected for public hearings. Perpetrators of violence could also give testimony and request amnesty from both civil and criminal prosecution.

The TRC, the first of the nineteen held internationally to stage public hearings, was seen by many as a crucial component of the transition to full and free democracy in South Africa. Despite some flaws, it is generally (although not universally) thought to have been successful.[3] The Institute for Justice and Reconciliation was established in 2000 as the successor organisation of the TRC.

Truworths is one of South Africa's leading fashion retailers and has the following brands in its stable.

U

Umkhonto we Sizwe means Spearhead of the Nation.

V

The **Vuvuzela** is a plastic horn, about 65 centimetres (2 ft) long, which produces a loud monotone note. Some models are made in two parts to facilitate storage, and this design also allows pitch variation. The intensity of these output depends on the blowing technique and pressure exerted.

X

Xenophobia. Since the end of apartheid and the opening of South Africa's borders in early 1990s, migrants from all over the world, especially African countries, have flocked to the southern African nation's cities and towns looking to escape the poverty and political intolerance in their home countries.

People from outside view South Africa as a place of opportunity but with the country's economy in stagnation, strained by an already high unemployment rate, tensions between local residents and foreign nationals have escalated in recent years. And this was not the first time, the xenophobic attacks of 2008 left more than 60 people, mostly foreign nationals, dead.

Y

Ya (Afrikaans, *Ja*) an expletive Yes!

Yong (Afrikaans: *Jong*). A young person, usually a young male such as a younger brother or son.

Z

Zulu. The Zulu people are, an ethnic group of southern Africa.